Contents

Chapter 1

ARE YOU A BOY BOFFIN?

So you think you know about boys? The mostly bewildering, sometimes smelly and occasionally dirty other half of the human race. But did you know that boys' changeable behaviour – although it seems often inexplicable – is often because, just like you, they're finding they have a rough deal when that delightful phase called 'puberty' kicks in? It's in the interest of your snog prospects, sanity and the ultimate destiny of mankind that you get smart on them. Honestly, it's easier than you think . . . So before we dig deep into the wonderful world of boys, let's see how much of a boy boffin you really are in this true or false quiz:

1 Boys have more of the oestrogen hormone than girls.   T☐ F☐

2 In general, girls start puberty earlier than boys.   T☐ F☐

3 Boys and girls have the same proportion of body fat.   T☐ F☐

4 Boys are more likely to suffer from acne than girls.   T☐ F☐

5 A penis is a muscle.   T☐ F☐

6 Boys can have erections before they reach puberty.   T☐ F☐

7 The left testicle hangs lower than the right one.   T☐ F☐

8 Girls have an Adam's apple.   T☐ F☐

9 All willies grow to the same size.   T☐ F☐

10 Willies that bend to the left or right are deformed.   T☐ F☐

How many did you get right?

1 F 2 T 3 F 4 T 5 F 6 T 7 T 8 T 9 F 10 F

3 and under: Boy blank

Boys are an alien species to you. You've spent most of your life living in blissful ignorance about them, but now you realise boys are a fundamental fixture so it's time to wise up on their bodies and their bizarre behaviour. So read on . . .

4 – 6: Boy basic

You know the basics but you're keen to uncover more about what makes boys tick. You're pretty sure they are from this planet but sometimes the way they act leaves you bothered and bewildered. Arming yourself with more info can only work to your advantage.

7 and over: Boy boffin

You're obviously wide awake in your biology classes as you've got a good working knowledge of what boys and girls experience when they hit puberty. On a personal level you're not always totally confident about dealing with boys and their puberty problems, but you're a quick learner.

Chapter 2

LOST IN PUBERTY

This puberty lark's a confusing business. OK, so girls have periods to cope with and all the painful and bizarre stuff that goes with them. But being a girl is great: at least you can talk, laugh and cry with your mates, read about what's normal and what isn't in *Bliss* features and problem pages, see the doctor if you're worried about anything, or even turn to Mum with your teen traumas.

So pity boys who often have nothing, no one, zero, zilch amount of help to get them through the minefield of manly growth. When it comes to boys and puberty, they're about as likely to discuss their problems or anxieties with their mates or their parents as they are to take up evening classes in flower arranging.

Boys don't get periods, so their puberty doesn't have an official start date. In comparison with girls, boys' body changes are gradual, but you can't ignore the physical fact that their bodies are undergoing some very radical refurbishment when puberty comes a-tapping on their bedroom door. And to get to grips with where boys are coming from you need to know one simple word: testosterone.

Testosterone is the male sex hormone and it's mega-powerful stuff. Once this hormone starts being released (usually around the ages of thirteen or fourteen) it wreaks havoc, both physically and emotionally. And the effects every smart girl needs to know about are:

1 The physical effect testosterone has on his penis and his body generally.

2 The emotional and psychological effects of puberty on a boy's mind.

3 The special lifelong relationship every boy develops with his beloved willy and its adjoining bits . . .

Chapter 3

THE WORLD OF THE WILLY

It may only be a few inches long, but you should never underestimate the important role the penis plays when it comes to understanding boys and their baffling behaviour.

So why does a piece of flesh which has been hanging around the front of his body for the first thirteen years of his life suddenly become the centre of his universe? And what part does testosterone play in this?

TACKLE TRAUMAS

During puberty, much to a boy's great pleasure, his willy gets bigger and thicker. Exactly how big and thick will be a constant source of anxiety to him well into his adult life, but there's nothing he can do to change it and, generally, there's not a lot of difference between most penis sizes.

Here are some basic willy facts:

• The average willy is usually between 6cm and 10cm long when it's soft and floppy (that's flaccid, if you want to use the technical term), and 13cm to 19cm when erect. And as for thickness, an erect penis is somewhere between 3–4cm across (in diameter).

• The penis is made of body tissue, full of blood vessels. When a boy is aroused blood pumps into the vessels and the penis becomes erect (i.e. a hard-on).

• At the tip of the willy is the head or glans. This is the most sensitive part of the willy, especially at the rim, which is the join between the head and the main bit of the willy – the shaft.

• Covering the glans is a fold of skin called the foreskin. This fold of skin protects the head of the willy, though if a boy's been circumcised for medical or religious reasons then this stretchy piece of skin will have been removed.

Circumcision

This is a common form of surgery, normally performed on babies for either religious, hygienic or cultural reasons. Sometimes it's performed on teenagers or even adults but only when there's a medical reason, e.g. it's painful when he tries to pull his foreskin back.

Some people believe a circumcised willy is healthier and cleaner than an uncircumcised willy. Defenders of circumcision claim there's no chance of any boy getting smegma under his foreskin if it's been removed.

Smegma or as some boys call it rather poetically, 'knob cheese', is a rather potent whitish, waxy discharge that smells rank if left to fester under the foreskin. But it's nothing regular showers or baths can't wash away.

Some men reckon a willy with a foreskin is more sensitive to touch as it still has its protective skin. But proud circumcised willy owners will swear there's no difference. Basically though, a willy's a willy and does all the same things whether it's got a foreskin or not.

His ball skills

Another major part of a boy's genitals is, of course, his balls (testicles/testes). These produce and store his sperm, and are held in a bag of skin called the scrotal sac (scrotum). A boy will first notice something weird happening when his balls slowly get bigger and start to hang lower. (When, at puberty, the testicles start producing semen, these millions of microscopic sperm need to be nice and cool, so the testicles move further away from the body: too close and sperm could get too hot and would not be fertile. When a boy gets cold or sexually excited the balls get firmer and pull themselves up towards his body, but when he warms up again or relaxes, they relax too!)

Over time a boy's balls will get bigger and the skin gets saggier and goes a darker shade than the rest of his body. By the time they've finished developing all boys tend to have one testicle hanging slightly lower than the other one. (This is usually the left one. Apparently it's to stop the balls bashing into each other when a boy's being physically active.)

Just like us, when we're convinced one boob

looks bigger than the other or seems to be growing faster than the other, boys panic when their balls appear to be uneven too. This is just a growth spurt and by the time they can safely call themselves 'men' things have usually equalled themselves out.

Wet dreams

Most boys are a bit bewildered by this puberty lark, but when they start to have wet dreams their worries get a lot worse. One morning a boy'll wake up, look down at his pyjama bottoms and, with a growing sense of horror, realise there's a sticky patch on his pjs: a gooey dollop of semen. He's just had his first wet dream.

For a lot of boys a wet dream can be the first time they've ever ejaculated, and some of them are so surprised they're convinced they've wet the bed or there's something seriously wrong with their willy. But actually, wet dreams show that there's nothing wrong at all, and that everything's in perfect working order.

Most boys will experience wet dreams between the ages of twelve to fifteen, but there's no hard and fast rule to these emissions. Some boys will never, ever experience them, while others will boast to their mates about how many they have in a week. A big myth about wet dreams is that it means a boy's a right pervert enjoying saucy dreams and this is what makes him ejaculate while he's asleep. But more often than not, they happen with absolutely no assistance from his dreams. Basically, it's just the body's way of emptying a boy's semen stores, so it can replenish with a fresh new stock of millions and millions of wriggling, jiggling sperm in his testes.

Depending on the boy himself, his response to wet dreams can be embarrassed, guilt-ridden or ecstatic, but as a girl, you'll never know. Boys would rather wear a miniskirt and have a perm than admit to a girl the existence of wet dreams, let alone if they're having them or not.

Embarrassing erections

Teenage boys are the masters of the universe when it comes to having erections any time, any place, anywhere. But it's not like they take a perverted pleasure out of this biological phenomena, or that they plan for it to happen just as they're getting off the number thirty-four bus.

The truth is, boys have no control over their

wayward willies, and it really doesn't matter if they're thinking about advanced maths or drooling over *FHM*. If a willy feels like popping up to say hello, then pop up it will.

It's highly embarrassing, very unwelcome and mostly uncomfortable for a boy when he's got a hard-on and there's nowhere for him to hide. So, if you're talking to him and he's started squirming, has gone bright red and insists on walking with his bag strategically positioned in front of him, chances are he's doing his very best to conceal his manhood.

Morning glories

If there's a time when most males are at the mercy of their wayward willy, it's first thing in the morning, when many of them wake up with a hard-on. No one really knows why this happens and what it all means, but some reckon a boy can have up to six erections a night when he's fast asleep. The morning wake-up call will subside quite quickly, the same as any other hard-on, either if he ignores it or if he masturbates to relieve it.

Masturbation mania

When a boy realises his willy is in full working order and, more to the point, the infinite pleasure he can get from playing with himself there's no stopping him – masturbating becomes a major pastime.

Masturbating and teenage boys are inextricably linked like salt and vinegar – it's the perfect pairing. Girls aren't supposed to know this: just like wet dreams and embarrassing erections, there's no way any boy will volunteer the info that he's pulling his plonker.

So, you're now either **a** disgusted, **b** laughing or **c** gobsmacked. But masturbating is a natural part of boys' growing up and discovering all about their bodies – honestly. It's a much-needed release for their sexy thoughts, fantasies and frustrations when their hormones and sexual urges are going ballistic. Quite frankly, the jaw-dropping fact behind all this masturbation business is the sheer frequency with which boys'll play with themselves. It can vary from once to up to five or six times a day. Some boys even play wanking games with their mates ('circle jerks'), usually along the lines of the first one to come is the winner!

So how does he do it? Well, he holds his willy in his hand and he rubs it up and down in a fury until he comes (ejaculates), probably into tissues, toilet paper or a hankie. The last thing he wants is for his mum to find semen-stained bedsheets.

When boys come the intensity can vary quite a lot (and it usually depends on how often or how recently they've masturbated) but normally the first ejaculation of the day will pump out vigorously. (If you'd like a visual demonstration of projectile sperm just rent out the video *There's Something About Mary* for that classic masturbation moment.)

THAT'S AMAZING!

If you examined a drop of semen about the size of a pinhead under a microscope you'd find about 1,500 sperm wriggling around. When a boy comes, he squirts out on average a teaspoonful of semen containing something like 300 million sperm.

The last one of the day can be a pathetic little dribble of semen. And it's not just its acrobatic abilities that can vary: even the colour and texture of milky-looking semen (with its millions of baby-making sperm swimming in it) can vary. Sometimes it can be quite thick and have a yellowy colour, and at other times it can be paler or creamier, or thin and watery.

Despite the fact that masturbating is perfectly natural and everyone does it, many boys feel very anxious or guilty about it. They may be afraid of splurting their seed all over the bedroom walls, of being caught in the act, or may just feel that, because they are so aware of it, everyone must be able to tell that they have been wanking. Some lads feel guilty that they're tossing off far too much and may be causing themselves some long-term damage. Of course, this is a load of utter rubbish, just like girls don't damage themselves through masturbation.

However, despite the worries that go along with it, boys find masturbating massively exciting and satisfying – and they never really grow out of it. Every adult male, no matter how often they're having sex, will still love to have the odd hand job.

WILLY WORRIES

With their daily 'examinations' of their willies, is it any wonder that your average boy doesn't stop worrying about his willy? There's the shape of it, the size of it, whether it's in full working order, and not to mention any random moles, warts and spots.

The bends

A bendy knob will only be obvious when he's got a stiffy and may frighten the pants off him when he first notices he hasn't got a 'ramrod' erection. But practically all willies have a curvy bend upwards and quite a number of them have a bit of a bend or a lean to either the left or right. This doesn't mean a boy is a freak or he'll never be able to have sex properly (some boys do worry that they've done themselves an injury with overzealous masturbation). However most boys – unless they're really confident and adventurous types – never see another erect willy, apart from their own, so they won't realise that other erections are the same. And practically no boy would ever admit to having an anxiety of this nature!

In very rare cases, a bendy penis can be a problem: there's a medical condition called Peyronie's disease, named after the French doctor who discovered it over two hundred years ago. It's when the curve or angle of a willy is so acute that an erection causes excrutiating pain. No one knows why this occurs, but somehow the tissue inside the penis, which is usually spongy, gets covered in scar tissue, and this stops it expanding normally and painlessly.

This is so rare though that it's a very, very unlucky boy who's ever struck down with this. Fortunately, it can sometimes be sorted out with skin grafts and surgery.

A spot of bother

Yes, even willies get spotty. In fact, it's very common and normal, and although boys tend to think their life is over as soon as they spot one (!) most spots disappear by themselves. Little pimples, lumps and bumps can pop up anywhere on the willy and balls and are usually just tiny hair follicles or sweat glands beginning to appear. What panics most boys is that they can look like a weird sort of whitish, creamy rash, but it soon settles down.

A warty one

A wart attack is in the Premiership of willy worries. But again it's quite common. Warts can attack in clusters or in a solitary assault and they can appear anywhere. Sometimes a wart can be so small it's hardly detectable, or it can be a big, lumpy one or a really painful stingy one. Some genital warts are sexually transmitted but a boy can be a virgin and still get them.

Treating a warty dick is the same as treating warts on any part of the body. His doctor may recommend a paint-on lotion, laser treatment or even that he has the warts frozen off. But what no boy with a warty willy should ever do is have sex. This is just asking for trouble as any genital warts can be passed on to girls and can cause cervical cancer.

WILLY WISDOM

I guess it's a bit obvious by now. But nothing, absolutely nothing, not even the defeat of his footie team in the dying seconds of an FA Cup Final, has a bigger impact on a boy's psyche than his most treasured possession: his willy. If he suspects his willy is woefully inadequate it'll whittle away at his self-esteem. And as most boys won't actually talk to anyone about their fears, worries and anxieties, they often are very defensive, secretive and uptight about their poor private parts and the problems of puberty.

His willy, aka . . .
Boys amuse themselves for
hours with this lot:

knob	**dong**	**love truncheon**
dick	**weener**	**penisweenie**
rod	**chopper**	**John Thomas**
prick	**beef**	**sausage**
tackle	**todger**	**whanger**
cock	**schlong**	**bazooka**
tool	**one-eyed trouser snake**	

Chapter 4

THE OTHER BODY STUFF YOU SHOULD KNOW

Your average boy doesn't just have testosterone and willy problems to contend with. Puberty will also cause him to develop a squeaky voice, body odour, spots and the new experience of facial and body hair!

The hairy stuff

A scattering of bum fluff on a boy's upper lip is one of the first telltale signs of puberty. This'll become thicker over a few years, and the hair will spread to his chin, jawline and lower cheeks.

As for the rest of his body, dark hair will sprout under his arms, round the base of his willy, over his chest, on his legs and sometimes even on his back and shoulders or bum! Body hair tends to be darker and coarser than facial hair, which means some lads will cultivate their own personal fleecy covering with impressive chest wigs.

Shaving stress

The appearance of a few straggly tufts of hair will get a boy very excited about the imminent prospect of shaving. Shaving is really important for boys – it's seen as a watershed between being a boy and being a man. Understandably, boys are always in a rush to be a man – a *real* man – so many of them spend hours practising in the bathroom mirror with their dad's razor, and many of them will shave for a long time before they *really* need to.

Zit alert

Boys often have more spots than girls as the hormone testosterone tends to give them greasy skin. It also gives them greasy hair, which can cause more spots if they let it flop into their faces. When boys suss out this link they usually develop an overwhelming fascination for personal hygiene and hair gel.

Pongarama

All the testosterone pumping through boys' bodies during puberty means that they will sweat buckets. Overactive sweat glands give boys smelly feet, sweaty armpits, a smelly bot and a sweaty body. So if they don't shower or bathe frequently boys can pong with body odour, big-time.

Luckily most young lads are supplied with an understanding, tactful mum (or even dad) who'll let him know it's about time he showered every day and used an anti-perspirant regularly, and that then, maybe one day, someone will get near enough to fancy him. This usually does the trick.

Beefing up

By the time a boy hits his late teens, his body will be developing into the body of a man. He'll grow taller, stronger and start to bulk out nicely. Unlike us girls, who are blessed with a greater proportion of body fat (that's what makes us all curvy, womanly and fleshsome), boys have little body fat and so look much more muscular than we ever can. All this means that a strapping young lad will start broadening out in the:

- **shoulders** – will broaden out. Mmm;

- **arms** – will become muscly and thicker. Yum;
- **chest** – broadens and expands. Lovely, and also
- **thighs** – become thicker and more muscular. Double mmm, yum and lovely.

A word of warning, though: this is when that squirt you used to beat up in primary school will suddenly shoot up into a walking, talking towerblock or bean-pole. At this point it's wise to stop teasing him!

The voice thing

Some boys suffer a great deal when their voices start breaking, so try not to laugh too heartily at them when it happens. One minute a boy'll be speaking normally; then his voice will crack and switch between a deeper sound and a squeak, completely without warning.

So why does this happen? It's because at puberty his larynx gradually gets bigger and his vocal chords become thicker and longer. At the same time it's this extension of his larynx, a hard bit of cartilage in his throat, that develops into a promi-nent Adam's apple. Some boys can be conscious of this as well, but don't tease them about it – you've got one too, it's just that yours doesn't show.

Chapter 5

Q & A: BOYS' BODY FREAK-OUTS

Occasionally boys will pluck up the courage to ask about their puberty problems. Some of the letters we receive at *Bliss* magazine show that they're as anxious and self-conscious as any girl. Read on, for an insider's look at teenage boy traumas:

Pizza face

I'm really spotty and have no self-confidence at all. Every time I go out I just want to hide my face from everyone. I'm sure girls must think I'm really ugly and dirty.

Boys really were at the front of the queue when the spot quota was being allocated, so don't worry – you're not alone! First of all, see your doctor and get your spots checked out. If you're suffering from severe acne there are topical applications you can use to help clear them up. If you've got a mild outbreak try spot treatments like Neutrogena from your local chemist. Keep your face clean and also keep your hair as clean as possible so no grease spreads from that to your face. And, however tempting it is, never ever pick your zits, and try not to touch your face too much: this will encourage other spots to appear as you spread the germs around. Slowly you'll see an improvement and as a result your confidence will build. As for girls thinking you're ugly and dirty because you've got a few spots, that's rubbish! Girls would prefer clean skin to kiss but it's personality that wins every time, so start dazzling them with yours and no one will notice your spots.

Little willy

I'm convinced my willy is too small. All my mates go on about how big their knobs are, and there's no way I'm as big as them. Is there anything I can do to make it bigger? I'm really depressed.

Every boy worries about the size of his willy, but the truth is that every single willy is different, and

THE SMART GIRL'S GUIDE TO **BOYS**

sizes vary. The usual length range is from six to 10 centimetres when it's floppy, and from 13 to 19 centimetres when erect – the average is 15 centimtres (that's six inches). And as for stretching it out a bit, well there's really nothing you can do about this. You may come across adverts for miracle devices or lotions or potions, but they won't change anything; basically you're stuck with what you've got. The important thing to remember is that it's not the size which matters but what you do with it. So stop worrying.

Masturbation mania

I'm really worried that I masturbate too much. Sometimes I'll do it more than once a day, and I'm afraid that if I continue like this I'm going to run out of sperm! Should I start doing it less often?

There's absolutely no need to be worried on this front, so relax and enjoy. Each of your testicles makes an average of two thousand sperm per second – that's two hundred million sperm every single day! You can masturbate as much as you like, there's no chance of running out as you'll constantly be producing a new supply.

Chapter 6

THE EMOTIONAL WORLD OF BOYS

If you look at yourself, your mates and all the girls you know you see that you're all different: shy, confident, funny, bitchy, insecure, mature, childish, sorted, paranoid . . . and a million different combinations of these things. Moreover the same person can change from day to day depending on hormones, moods, who they're with, what's been happening – loads of things constantly affect how you feel and sometimes you may feel you're on a rollercoaster of changing emotions!

Well, it may not surprise you to know that boys are a mixture of all these things too. And the anxieties you feel about being popular or fanciable, or about your changing body . . . boys feel all these too! The biggest difference is that hardly any boys will reveal their true feelings and worries to anyone.

It's a sad fact that boys who blab their feelings or, worse still, cry are viewed with great suspicion by their fellow males. It's a brave lad indeed who'll acknowledge that, 'No, actually I'm feeling a bit insecure about myself today,' when greeted by one of his mates with the customary, 'All right, mate?'

Apparently it's not big, tough, cool or clever to let it all hang out. At this point in their lives, most boys are trying really hard to be *men* and they are horribly conscious about displaying any so-called 'weakness' or vulnerability – and this includes having feelings. Some boys are so hung up about it that they reckon boys who do show glimmers of sensitivity must be gay. What these boys don't realise is that **a** being gay is perfectly normal and doesn't make you less of a man, and **b** it's OK to show your emotions.

Thankfully there are plenty of boys who realise there's nothing wrong with having emotions and talking about them (if you want to, of course) and there's absolutely nothing wrong with being gay (and that talking about emotions and being gay aren't necessarily related). Some boys may be a bit defensive about their feelings; they may never own up to doubts and fears and may act over the top to hide what's really going on. But with good friends, or people they have come to trust, some of them will open up a bit – and they may find it helps.

WHAT'S IN HIS HEAD?

Lads, although they'd hate you to realise this, are a walking, talking bundle of insecurities. They too spend hours alone in their bedrooms anxiously contemplating these horrific questions:

1 Am I the ugliest boy in the universe?
2 Will a girl ever fancy me?
3 Am I too short?
4 Am I too hairy? Or not hairy enough?
5 Will girls laugh when they see me in my swimming shorts?

6 How do you make the first move?

7 How do I ask a girl out?

8 What if she says 'no'?

9 Will my mates laugh at me?

10 How do I join the Foreign Legion?

So what are a boy's major preoccupations and, more importantly, how can understanding his fixations help you understand him?

Mirror, mirror . . .

It's a well-known fact that boys love to tease girls about how long they take to get ready to go anywhere. But many guys are just as guilty as us of spending hours in the bathroom or bedroom preening themselves to perfection. The big difference is that they spend hours endeavouring to achieve the this-is-what-I-look-like-when-I've-just-got-out-of-bed effect. Don't believe it for a second: every boy has an image he's gagging to project and whether it's the floppy-haired or super-gelled one it still means a great deal to him.

Added to this, and his worries about spots, a lad will be petrified of looking any less than how he thinks a *real* man should look, which means most of them are really worried about looking too skinny or too baby-faced. It's the same if they have to wear glasses or braces: boys are paranoid they'll end up the town idiot and class joke and, worse still, that every girl in a fifty-kilometre radius will crack up as soon as they see him.

Boys also take their clothes very seriously. You can safely bet that 99.9% are still letting their mums buy their undies, but at least by the age of fifteen they've usually taken full responsibility for the rest of their wardrobe. A boy's dream scenario is for everyone to be suitably impressed by his natural style and sartorial elegance, so he goes for the I'm-so-cool-I've-just-thrown-this-stuff-together look. Again, this is another boy myth. It takes hours of preparation to achieve this before he'll tippy-toe out of his front door.

Top tip: Boys are infinitely less cool, secure and confident than they'd like you to think, especially when there are girls around. Which makes it really easy for you to convince any lad what a lovely, considerate person you really are. Just utter a throw-away remark when you get the opportunity, like, 'Hey, don't you look cool in that jacket!' He'll be forever grateful and a lot more comfortable in your company: and if he feels less pressure to prove himself and impress you he might be a bit more himself, which can only be a good thing. Just don't snigger when you pay a compliment as this'll destroy him and your chances along with it.

Macho message

You can't blame boys for their bizarre behaviour, as it's often not entirely their fault. Boys receive completely mixed messages from society. They're still expected to be strong, macho, fearless and competitive, and they're bombarded with images of the hunky, tough man who can cope with everything alone, but there's also pressure on them to be a 'new' lad and display their caring, sharing side. Most are probably very confused by this whole business, and have no idea what's expected of them or will gain approval, so if they seem to be over-the-top try to be patient – but don't feel you need to be impressed by any macho behaviour!

Top tip: Pretend you haven't noticed the boy racer stripes tattooed on his forehead or his tales of his alarming latest exploits and sooner or later he'll realise he's not impressing you and will drop the act.

He has to be sooo cool

You know what really keeps a boy awake at night? It's complete terror of being relegated to the loser league of life. All boys dream of being the coolest guy in town. Of course, the degrees of coolness can vary according to the individual. Some work hard at cultivating the rebellious, 'I'm so misunderstood', moody cool. Mainly because they've twigged that all girls are suckers for this one, and other guys are impressed with it. However very few achieve this level.

Other levels of cool in a boy's world are attained by being good at:

- sports or sports trivia,
- computer games,
- wearing the right clothes and trainers,
- getting into really obscure music and spending a small fortune on overpriced import tracks,
- having a car (preferably sporty-looking),
- drinking beer,
- buying all the latest gadgets (boys adore gadgets, without exception),
- dating a girl (but absolutely no public displays of affection allowed).

Top tip: It's a fine line between a cool dude and a sad anorak. Some boys will humour themselves for months on end trying to be the most skilled player ever to hold a Dreamcast, or to impress their mates with their knowledge of every footie result since 1891. Don't worry though: when you get to know them, most boys relax a little and realise they don't have to impress you twenty-four hours a day. This is when you can get to know the real boy.

Chapter 7

BOYS WITH THEIR MATES

Most boys are so anxious that even if they get to the point of feeling relaxed with you and letting you get to know the person beneath the facade, there's a good chance they'll start acting very strangely when their mates show up.

On their lonesome, most lads have the ability to be the cutest, sweetest soul on the planet. They'll suddenly reveal the ability to string sentences together – shock, horror! Any boy with a brain cell in his head secretly relishes the opportunity to show off his social skills with a girl, especially if he quite fancies her.

Unfortunately as soon as any of his mates show up round the corner with a chorus of 'Oy, Sam, all right, mate!' it's a signal to his brain to mutate into that of a lad. He'll develop a talent called 'selective vision' which translates as he'll blank you. This is followed a nanosecond later by him shuffling off with 'the lads', as they affectionately thrash the living daylights out of him. Why? Because most boys are petrified their mates will give them a hard time in front of girls.

So what exactly's going on? It's time to deconstruct the basic components of male bonding.

1 - The group mentality

While battling the traumas and insecurities of being a teenager most boys are desperate for reassurance and security. Just think of them as a harmless flock of sheep: it really is safety in numbers for them, and that's why they love to hang out in gangs.

Boys, while fascinated, are also secretly petrified of girls, and they congregate together to offer each other some macho male support and spend their time pretending girls are the last thing on their minds.

However there is another side to the group thing: the pressure to conform is overwhelming and every boy lives in fear of being ridiculed by his mates, which leads to . . .

2 – Teasing torture

Loads of boys tease their mates mercilessly if one of them shows any signs of 'irregular' behaviour. Top behavioural patterns guaranteed to be ridiculed are:

1 fancying a girl;
2 talking to the girl he fancies;
3   expressing his feelings or anxieties;
4 crying (or even looking like he's about to blub), and
5 getting all touchy-feely with his mates.

It's not just behaving differently that'll make him a prime target for humiliation. If he's too skinny, fat, short, tall, spotty, brainy, ugly, smelly, stupid, wears glasses/braces or both, has greasy hair, stutters or lisps, he'll expect to get ribbed by his mates about stuff, most of which is beyond his control.

Most boys grow out of this behaviour fairly quickly or find a new bunch of like-minded mates who just accept them for who they are. But this teasing reflects boys' insecurity and defensiveness, and also another major part of boy friendships – their macho competitive streak.

3 - The 'I'm the best' syndrome

Boys simply can't admit to their mates that they're worried about things – especially girls, or about their own emerging masculinity – so often they'll over-compensate by bluffing badly with the most ridiculous macho behaviour. However many boys also share one fatal flaw: their competitive streak. It probably hasn't escaped your notice (maybe when your little bro' stomps out of the room every time you beat him on PlayStation) that boys hate to lose – anything.

Most boys just can't help themselves in the game of one-upmanship, from the best farter or burper, to computer whizz or even king of the willies. Boys love to brag about how great they are: they simply can't help showing off. And if – oh my God! – one of them snogs a girl, it's part of the male code to go back to their mates and brag about that too. This is when boys are honour-bound to exaggerate every encounter they've had with a girl. So if this does happen to you, do try not to take it too personally – put it down to this boy's immaturity, and walk away.

Most boys, however, aren't very comfortable conforming to this behaviour all the time and will eventually stop being so competitive, usually when they're starting to feel relaxed about themselves and about being in your company.

4 - The girl thing

With mates monitoring their every move, most lads have to play a fine balancing act if they want to look 'popular' with girls. The ultimate macho status symbol is to flirt and be seen hanging out – in a dead cool way, of course – with the 'fanciable' girls: those drop-dead gorgeous girls with a string of drooling boys traipsing behind them wherever they go. But don't give up if your dream boy's conforming to this predictable pattern; he knows just as well as you that Ms Fancy-Pants is unattainable because she's either: **a** already in a steady relationship with a boy who's years older, or: **b** she's years older, and his English or Art student teacher.

Another big factor in this fine juggling act between his mates and girls is a boy's ultimate dread of looking like a rejected fool. What boy in his right mind would pluck up the courage to ask a girl out if he has any suspicions that she'll blow him out? Oh the humiliation. It would be unbearable for him.

43

Many boys, even if they've been mates with girls for years, find that the issue of sexuality changes everything and they can't figure out how it's all going to work with this new dimension. Even friendship can seem impossible and, confused and uptight, they may revert to childish teasing, bravado or really distant behaviour for a while. It just takes time for them to sort out their own lives and to get used to these new, more adult relationships with girls.

5 - Boytalk

Firstly, let's get one thing straight. Stop wasting your time wondering what that guy you're mad for really talks about when he's alone with his mates. Sorry, but you're not missing out on any of life's great mysteries.

The thing with most boys is that they don't talk about any topics we think are important and, what's more, they don't talk in a language we'd immediately recognise.

We already know there's massive pressure on a boy not to reveal his true feelings when he's in his gang. That means certain topics are avoided altogether. OK, so they'll talk about who fancies who, and who's snogged who, but it'll be done in a strictly superficial and jokey way, and all the time they'll be teasing each other, showing off and putting each other down.

Boytalk is a peculiar language that they make their own. It will usually consist of a few key catchphrases, like 'All right?', 'Sorted', 'Respect', 'Fierce', and 'Lush'. Boys take great delight in stripping the English language down to its bare minimum and then grunting these words to one another at sporadic intervals. They'll also spend hours of fun reciting hilarious catchphrases and TV/movie lines at each other. The sillier and more repetitive, the better. All this makes them think they're part of an exclusive club, as no one can understand a word they're saying. It's a 'belonging' thing.

Of course, some boys might talk with their best mate about a heavy thing they're going through, like their parents divorcing or a family bereavement. But generally when you're out with boys, talk of any seriously heavy topics is strictly prohibited.

To girls, this may sound totally mental, but most boys are so paranoid about looking 'cissy' that they'll risk being miserable inside, just so they can appear like a 'real man' on the outside. As they get older, though, most boys realise it's 'good to talk' and get less hung-up about looking unmasculine (which was never the case anyway). It's just a shame that some boys never learn to open up.

6 - The hilarious world of boys

The top ten of what's a scream in boys' strange lives . . .

1 Reciting Ali G – *ad infinitum.*

2 Inflicting great physical pain on each other.

3 Farting.

4 Burping.

5 Anything to do with periods, boobs and bums.

6 Whatever the coolest one in the gang thinks is funny.

7 Drinking lots . . . and passing out.

8 Making revolting jokes about each other.

9 Calling each other 'gay boy'.

10 When you trip up in the street.

Chapter 8

BOY TYPES AND HOW TO COPE WITH YOUR CRUSH

Even though boys sometimes seem strange, that doesn't stop us from fancying them like crazy. And as you learn more about them you find that there are many different types of boy. So before you waste any more valuable time day-dreaming about your crush boy, and engineering the perfect opportunity to wow him with your personality, you need to suss out what makes him tick. Once you've uncovered this vital info on the different types of boy, it'll be much easier to make him notice you. Now let's get boy-savvy . . .

THE 7 CLASSIC GUY TYPES

1 – The footie freak

What makes him tick?: He never takes off his favourite team's strip, and will proudly show off his footie memorabilia to any unsuspecting soul. Footie is his obsession, but this lad will have a sport to follow for every season – he'll even watch golf if he's that desperate.

You'll rarely find this boy alone. If he's not safely surrounded by his equally footie-obsessed mates, always talking footie trivia, you'll find him on the nearest playing field seriously believing he's Michael Owen incarnate. When the realisation hits that he isn't, he'll retire (with all his mates) to the sanctuary of his bedroom and Sky Sports One.

How to cope: You could bribe your mates into forming a cheerleaders group: it's guaranteed to get you in your dream boy's field of vision for a few hours every week. And, as for the away games, imagine all those ever-so-casual chitchat opportunities on the numerous coach trips.

On the other hand, the footie freak admires devotion and passion, so you could get going with your own interests and hobbies – nothing impresses a boy like a girl with a talent and real purpose to her life. Or, alternatively, if you really can't stand sport or him talking about it you may have to direct your attentions to another boy.

2 - The cool kid

What makes him tick?: This boy type usually falls into two subtypes. **a** is the loner indie kid. He's the extremely pale-looking one who insists on sitting alone in class, staring moodily out of the window – all day long. He likes to rebel by experimenting with strange hair dyes and styles, and has a strong liking for black nail polish. He'll skulk all over town with just one or two close mates, usually to HMV, and swiftly back to one of their bedrooms to listen to the latest Japanese import of a band no one else even cares about. **b** This indie kid is way more sociable than his close relation. He's into all the latest labels and trends, and has a merry band of followers to show off his carefully-acquired skills, whether it's skateboarding or breakdancing. He has to be acknowledged as cooler than a freezer by all his mates.

How to cope: The trouble with this type is that they've taken self-obsession to the max. He's either too off in his own wacky world (see subtype **a**) to even notice the existence of the female sex or he's far too busy maintaining his cool status to spare any time for girls (see subtype **b**).

But what these boys both need is chill-out time, and that's where you come in. You can engage them in conversation by asking them about the stuff they're into and then, once they feel relaxed in your company and are opening up, you can start talking about the stuff you like. They may not agree with your taste or style but they'll definitely respect a girl who at least knows her own mind.

3 - The funny guy

What makes him tick?: He's the class clown, the one who can always be relied upon to lighten the atmosphere just before you sit those pesky end-of-term exams.

You'll never find this boy on his lonesome: he's forever going round backslapping everyone as if they're dear old mates. And the big dilemma? He's far too busy concocting his next hilarious line to even suspect someone fancies him.

How to cope: This guy is desperate for attention and reassurance, and all you have to do to get him to notice you is – laugh. It's so easy. If you fancy yourself as a bit of a comedian you could challenge him to a comedy stand-off. However this runs the risk of upstaging him, and there's nothing an insecure boy fears more than the real threat of being upstaged by a *girl*. Maybe it's best just to keep on laughing.

4 - The arty-farty one

What makes him tick?: It could be music, drama, painting, writing or acting. Whatever gets this guy going certainly dominates his life both in and out of school. He'll hang out with like-minded people and has little patience for anyone else. He constantly believes he's misunderstood, and if his creative bag is his 'rock' band, then he's probably right.

How to cope: You'll need to be dedicated to his interests to get a look-in with this one. You're on to a winner if you happen to be into the same stuff as him, but you'll need to be a saint and sacrifice a lot of your own social life to keep up with him. The key to plucking this guy's heartstrings is, as well as showing an interest in *him*, to show you're creative and independent yourself.

5 - The popular lad

What makes him tick?: This boy is not only nice to everyone, he's even Mr Nice to his teachers, but he does it in such a way he's still considered cool and everyone looks up to him. He's wise beyond his years and most lads go to him for advice, while practically every other girl is also drooling over this highly-motivated guy. Is there anything amiss with Mr Perfect? Er, nope.

How to cope: This one is a real achiever, but the trouble with the boy-who-can-do-no-wrong is you never really know what he thinks of you. Since he's super-lovely to everyone, how can you be so sure who he's into? The best strategy is to network: play him at his own game by joining in loads of activities. At least then you're bound to run up against him a few evenings a week. This is one boy who can't say no to a girl with her own opinions and a go-getting attitude, so just talk to him, have fun, let him get to know you and see what happens!

6 - The shy boy

What makes him tick?: Getting through the day without uttering a word to anyone but his close mates is what makes this boy tick. It's not that he relishes his bashful nature, he's just got so little self-confidence that he's absolutely terrified of looking like a fool in front of anyone. However often this brooding silence is only a disguise, and you may find that deep within him is a lovely, witty, smart boy gagging to show someone who he really is.

How to cope: It was probably the sexy silent side which really got your imagination working overtime, so you're fighting a double-edged sword with this one. You like him specifically because he doesn't exhibit the normal boy behaviour, but how will you ever get him to open his mouth and speak? Shy boys tend to operate best on a one-to-one basis so get him to communicate beyond the monosyllabic with a little bit of flattery when he's on his own. Find out what he's into and be there – find a project or activity in common so that you can meet through something. It'll take the focus and the pressure off your conversation and don't worry, he'll be glad you're even talking to him.

7 – The brainbox

What makes him tick?: There are two types of smartypants: the ones who work at it – the swots, and the ones who are natural-born brain-boxes. Whatever category your fancy boy falls in, it still equals a guy who loves an intellectual challenge and uses his time constructively. Swotting requires self-discipline, self-sacrifice, determination and dedication, so at least you know your dream boy has sterling qualities. The problem is getting this bookworm out of the library long enough to notice your sterling qualities.

How to cope: If you're a whizzkid at his chosen topic too, then you've already got an advantage when trying to steal him away from his study books. Alternatively you could explain how his after-school tuition would work wonders on your end-of-term prospects. Not only are you flattering him (not many boys can resist this) but you're also appealing to his grey matter by giving him an academic challenge. Any opportunity for stimulating conversation and debate will really get him hooked on you.

Chapter 9

A BOY'S VIEW OF A GIRL'S WORLD

It doesn't matter what category a boy falls under because there's a universal truth common to all of them: they're in total awe of you and your mates.

Of course, they'll never admit this. Privately though, most boys are dying to know more about the mysterious world of girls (why do you think your bro is forever thumbing through your latest issue of *Bliss*?). Boys are gagging for more info – any morsel, in fact, which may help them in their quest to look irresistible to us. Part of boys' fascination is also a secret, yearning jealousy: of the mysterious bond between girls, the way we can be in touch with our feelings, and how easy we find it to talk about our emotions. Unfortunately, boys gossip about the silliest things and end up spreading outrageous rumours about what we're really like and, worse still, most boys believe all the rubbish they tell each other and wind each other up horribly.

Consequently, boys are very uncomfortable with the mysteries of the female world. It's the same with all that period stuff: any mention of tampons, PMT, pads or lingerie will make them:

1 perform a Scooby dash in the opposite direction;

2 giggle and snigger uncontrollably, or

3 pretend these things don't exist.

Boys just can't help themselves when it comes to these intimate but so, so normal female things. They're really dead nosy about what's happening to your body, but they're too embarrassed to deal with it – which is why they resort to childish teasing or laddish jokes. They're not necessarily trying to be horrible; it's just that they can't cope.

There are also a few myths doing the rounds about our preoccupations. Some boys truly believe we're totally obsessed with boys, make-up, clothes, hair styles, boys, shoes, gossip and more boys. Er, well it's not quite like that, is it? Honestly, where do they get their silly ideas from!

WHAT MAKES BOYS DAZED & CONFUSED?

1 – The way we like 'nice' boys but only as friends

This drives most boys (who aren't naturally bad) crazy. There they are, trying to be as 'nice' as possible (I did say 'trying'), because Mum's always told them girls only like nice boys, and what do we do? Go totally loopy over the guy with the dodgy tattoos, a wicked smile and half the girls you know on his speed-dial option. Then we complain when all the sweet guys twig on to this and we're left with no one to help us with our homework. Oops.

2 – The way we cry whenever we feel like it

The thing with boys is that when someone's crying they suspect something's wrong, and if something's wrong, in their books, it needs to be fixed. But what can they do? Put their arm round you? But then you might guess they really like you! And that's not an option, is it? Which is why 99.9% per cent of boys will stand like idiots mortified with fear if a sobbing girl is anywhere near them. It's not that they're all insensitive gits, they simply don't know how to deal with these situations.

3 - The way we visit the toilets together

OK, so we love to gossip and there's no better place than in the loos with your best mate. But boys just don't get this; in their heads you go to the toilet, do what comes naturally and then leave, all executed in the space of forty-five seconds. Boys reckon our lengthy chitchats are rude and unnecessary but, more importantly, they also make them mega-paranoid.

4 - The way we tell our mates everything

It's probably one of the most fundamental differences between the sexes, that girls share everything with their closest mates, while boys share footie facts. It's easy for girls to spill the beans on our dreams, hopes, worries and anxieties, but if a boy tries to do that he faces the prospect of being ridiculed by his ever-so-understanding mates, or faces a stony silence full of cringeworthy tumble-weed moments followed by 'Er, right. So are you playing footie down the park this weekend?'

TEN THINGS THAT BAFFLE BOYS

1 How we consult our friends before making the most minor decision.

2 Why chocolate rules.

3 Our wild mood swings.

4 Why we have to plan everything.

5 How we always compare ourselves to every girl we know (and ones we don't know, for that matter).

6 That we love our manky-looking teddy.

7 How excited we get over stationery.

8 Our ability to talk on the phone for hours.

9 How we can never stop giggling – however hard we try.

10 Our fascination with shoes and hair clips.

Chapter 10

WHY BOY MATES ARE GOOD FOR YOU

Forget your masterplan of convincing the object of your lust that you're well and truly alive, just regroup for a sec because you may have the ultimate secret weapon right under your nose: a boy friend!

OK, so they're not always that easy to find, but apart from the burping and farting, having a boy as a really good friend is just what's needed when you're trying to decode your dream boy's bizarre behaviour. And another bonus never to be underestimated: a boy mate gives you unlimited access to all his mates if your dream dude turns into a dreary dud! It's a two-way relationship, of couse, because boys secretly love to chill out with a bunch of female friends – it's a welcome relief from all that competitive bravado boys insist on maintaining with each other. They also love to have female friends because:

1 they can confide in you without fear of ridicule;

2 it takes all that guesswork out of the mysterious world of girls;

3 it offers them access to all your gorgeous girlfriends, and

4 it makes other boys insanely jealous (i.e.: 'I have girls as friends, therefore I'm really, really mature and utterly cool and gorgeous.').

So, apart from an intimate knowledge of the Premiership's fixture list, what's really the upside of having a boy pal? Here are my ten golden reasons why you need a boy buddy . . .

1 – Instant dates

Got a posh dance or a family do on the horizon? Determined not to go as the terrible twosome with your best mate – yet again? Take your perfect boy pal instead! If he scrubs up well and has one decent jacket then you've got yourself a no-strings-attached, will-he-won't-he-kiss-me-at-the-end-of-the-night? perfect emergency date.

2 – Connections

You can get even closer to that guy you fancy if you're actually on speaking terms with one of his mates. But be careful, it's one of the oldest tricks in the book and you shouldn't take the mick too much and use your boy mate just so you get access and can dazzle 'the boy who must be yours' with your wit and charm. Boys aren't that stupid and will suss you out if using them is part of your game plan.

3 – Reality check

Boys are excellent if you want an honest opinion. The trouble with some girl friends is they're petrified of hurting your feelings or looking like a bitch, so they may not tell you the whole truth when you do in fact look like Ronald McDonald with that new lippy on. Boys, on the other hand, won't hesitate about breaking the bad news. But lay off the 'Does my bum look big in this?' questions – it's a lose–lose situation and they know it too.

4 - Free stuff

You've got no cash for a new CD or book, so what do you do? Pop over to boy mate's place and help yourself to whatever you fancy (forget his wardrobe though, most of his stuff will be on the floor). Boys are fantastic for borrowing clothes/ CDs/books, or indeed anything else you feel like liberating from his bedroom. Why? They're easily confused. So mention the 'objects on loan' every time you meet him, swear blind you'll return them the next time, then repeat this mantra for the next three years. Sorted.

5 - Behavioural studies

Having a boy mate gives you privileged access to the wonders of the boy world and gains you a first-hand, no-holds-barred insight to the worst side of them. At the time you may be thinking, 'Yuk, how on earth does he get his whole finger up that nostril?' But while he's inspecting his bogeys, he's also preparing you for a proper 'boyfriend'. Yes, even your lovegod will burp, fart and pick his nose too.

6 – Dibbo diverter

Everyone should have a boy pal, if only because they make amazingly accurate anti-doofus devices. When you're stuck in a corner, fending off the unwanted attentions of Mr Pepperoni-breath, you can rely on your very best boy friend to rescue you. Even if you do have to pretend you're 'together', nothing beats him in the idiot-repellent stakes.

7 – Your champion

Boys love to show off, we all know that, but what about when one's showing off by spreading rumours about *you*? That's when your boy bud saves the day. He'll shut up a lying toerag in a flash with a well-delivered, 'Sorry, mate. But that's my pal you're lying about, and you're spewing utter crap!' Nice one, boy friend!

8 – Roadtest dummy

They're great for practising all those flirting tricks you've so far only talked about with your girl mates. Boys love to watch girls do all their girlie stuff, and will be perfectly happy to let you try out that winning smile, sexy stare or that killer hairflick. Make the most of it, and ask for some feedback on your flirting techniques. At least you'll find out if that 'alluring' look actually makes you look bonkers.

9 – Dating tips

Friendship is a two-way thing and this means you'll probably be the first person your boy mate will turn to when he's got girl problems. So use the wisdom you'll gain about what makes boys bemused, bewildered or just blue, and then you're unlikely to fall into the same traps. You've got a hotline to what really makes a boy tick, so go dial his grey matter.

10 – Quality control

And finally, what about when you need boy help, but don't realise it? Guys are very, very protective about their girl pals. And if the boy you're mad about isn't right for you, for whatever reason, you can rely on your boy pal to tell you the truth. You might not like what you're hearing but you've got to respect it. He's got your best interests at heart, so listen up!

KEEPING IT PLATONIC

There's usually some degree of mutual attraction between male and female friends, but that doesn't mean you or he are secretly gagging to snog each other's faces off.

Some people believe it's impossible for a girl and a boy to be 'just good friends'; they reckon the two must secretly fancy each other. But the fact is you can be mates on a purely platonic level as long as you're mature and honest enough to carry it off.

If you suspect your boy pal fancies you, then you must proceed with caution. And however much it makes you squirm, be honest with him about your feelings. And don't drop him like a ton of bricks – he is your mate after all.

It's the same if you befriend a boy just because you secretly fancy the pants off him. Now you're playing a dangerous game with your heart. Here are the possibilities:

a He'll suss you out and tell you he just wants to be a mate.

b You'll eventually confess true love and he'll answer with option **a**.

c He'll start feeling uncomfortable hanging out with you, and make excuses about being too busy to meet up.

d He'll eventually get a girlfriend (not you), leaving you Little Ms Heartbroken.

Of course, some friendships do eventually develop into girlfriend/boyfriend relationships. Well, being his mate is a mighty fine way of sussing him out and of getting close, but don't bet on every boy pal as a potential boyfriend and don't make friends with boys just because you're mad about them. (And don't not become mates with a boy just because you don't fancy him.)

Oh, and watch out for any boy friends who are intent on snogging their way around all your girl mates. Now is he really your true friend or is he just using you? Mmm, tricky one that . . .

Chapter 11

Q & A: BOYS' EMOTIONAL FREAK-OUTS

Read on for insider info on boys' emotional doubts and dilemmas . . .

Cry baby

I'm really ashamed of myself. I cried in front of a girl I know and now I can't face seeing her again. I'm convinced she thinks I'm a wimp for blubbing.

Showing you're human and have strong emotions is nothing to be ashamed about. Chances are that since you were a little boy you've been brainwashed into thinking that crying is not cool and is something boys just don't do, but this is a load of rubbish: bottling up your feelings is much more harmful for your emotional and physical well-being. Most girls often have a good cry and are unlikely to ridicule you for doing the same. In fact, you'll probably be overwhelmed with sympathy and support, as girls suspect any boy who cries must have a pretty serious problem he is coping with and they'll also respect a boy who can express his emotions.

Unrequited love

I've been friends with a girl who lives next door to me for a few years. But now I think I've fallen for her. What should I do?

Being good friends with a girl and having a boyfriend/girlfriend relationship are totally different matters. You feel close to this girl because you obviously spend a lot of time together and get on both emotionally and socially, but don't confuse your feelings of closeness with romantic feelings. Also, she may only see you as a good mate, so firstly you need to have an honest chat with her and confess that your feelings for her have changed. It may be embarrassing for the two of you initially, but at least you'll know where you stand.

THE SMART GIRL'S GUIDE TO **BOYS**

Spod alert

I know I'm a bit of a brainy geek. But I'm really paranoid that every girl in school is laughing at me.

Don't ever be ashamed of who you are, and never underestimate the pulling power of the sexiest organ a boy has: his brain. During your teens, anyone who displays anything out of the ordinary is a target for teasing practice. But sensible people learn to appreciate that everyone has a special gift and will admire you for it. Stand proud and some girls will appreciate you for who you are, and as you get older, many more will be begging you for homework help, or just for some interesting company!

Bad boys

Why do girls fancy bad boys who are at least two years older than them? I'm quite quiet and worry no one'll ever fancy me.

Not all girls are crazy for boys who misbehave. It's just that some girls have a romantic notion that the rebellious ones are far more exciting to be with than sensible boys, and they're viewed as infinitely cooler too which makes them look very good in front of their mates. Some girls also believe they can change boys' wicked ways.

However by the time most girls have had their hearts broken several times by these types, they tend to steer clear of them. Which is where 'nice' boys like you step in to show them there are good lads in the world.

Gay feelings

I'm really worried that I fancy other boys. Every time we're in the school changing-room, I can't stop having sexual thoughts about my mates. Am I gay?
It's perfectly normal to experience these feelings while you're going through the trauma of puberty. It's a confusing, bewildering and emotional process. But this doesn't mean you'll always feel this way, so don't stress out. According to Jeremy Daldry's book, *Boys Behaving Badly*, one in three boys will get up to something sexual with another boy. It's all part of finding out your true sexual orientation. If you do eventually realise you're gay, try not to get stressed about that either; there's absolutely nothing wrong with it.

Chapter 12

THE SECRET SIGNS OF ATTRACTION

How do you discover if your dream lover's dreaming of you too? Well, you could risk total humiliation by getting your mates or even you (eek!) to: **a** ask his mates or **b** ask him.

Er, thought not.

Alternatively you can sharpen up your boy radar skills and you'll soon work out if he's transmitting the right signals. And how do you achieve this amazing feat? Easy! Boys are generally crap at flirting and can only operate on primitive levels. Here are their favoured damage-limitation pulling techniques and how to decode them:

Furtive glances

If he's noticed you he'll find it almost impossible to keep his eyes off you. This is a preferred strategy often employed by the quieter, less confident types. It's low-risk, i.e. no teasing from his mates, and you can easily let him know you're into him by holding his gaze for a couple of seconds. If you're brave you could even give him one of your cheeky little smiles. That's if he ever stops looking away quickly every time you catch him out.

Sneaky smiles

This is a step up from the staring-like-a-loon approach. He's obviously gaining in confidence, so give him further encouragement by smiling back at him and saying, 'Hi.' He'll be gobsmacked.

Teasing

Boys can't help teasing full stop. They tease their mates, they tease every girl they know. But the teasing will be totally over the top if a boy fancies you. Does he tease you about the way you look? Does he have a nickname for you? Does he have the hots for you? Yep.

Acting cool

Occasionally a boy may adopt a classically female approach of looking like he couldn't care if you are dead or alive. This method is a tough one to decode, as he may well feel the way he looks. You'll have to take the initiative and actually talk to this guy to suss out if he's interested. If he sticks around for longer than five minutes and maintains steady eye contact with you, it's looking good.

Showing off

Does your dream guy pop a wheelie on his bike every time he rides past you? Or does he suddenly start wrestling mates into hedges if he spots you walking down the street? Bless him, he's trying to prove his manhood to make you swoon.

Being horrible

If he's really insecure or thinks you don't fancy him, he could opt for the cringe factor every time he spots you. It's strange how boys think throwing insults at you will make you fancy them. Spooky.

Team effort

This strategy is available in two formats: **a** telling his mates he likes you, or **b** asking one of them to tell you he fancies you. This means he can suss out whether *you* like *him* from a safe distance, using his mates to filter out any possible embarrassing situations. His mates will make it their mission to see if you fancy him by either saying how great he is or saying he's a right dibbo, and judging how you react. And when he's reassured enough to send his mate over to deliever the immortal line 'My mate fancies you', tell his mate, 'That's great, but he's got to ask me out himself.'

Body language

Even if your dream boy is cooler than a fridge freezer, his body may give him away. If a guy is standing next to you with as much of his body turned towards you as possible that's an 'I like you' move. If he's sitting down, look out for his legs and feet pointing towards you. Touching his hair or face is another give-away, and if he's sitting directly opposite you with his hands on his thighs and his legs wide apart, he's definitely sexually attracted to you.

Other dead certs

Some of these signs may be too subtle or just plain impossible to read, but if you get to know a guy it'll get clearer. And there should be little hints . . .

• He remembers something you said to him three months ago.
• He teases you by asking where your 'boyfriend' is.
• He and his mates go out of their way to dance right next to you.
• He's always in the same place as you.
• He can never quite look you in the eye if you start talking to him.
• He makes like a lobster if you so much as smile at him.
• He knows where you live.
• He talks to you and only you in a packed-out house party (or indeed anywhere).
• He leaves you sweet notes in your locker.
• His mates poke him and snigger when you appear.
• He kisses you. Very obvious.

WHAT BOYS GO CRAZY FOR

He's generally very grateful to anyone who's remotely interested in him, so unless you're Jabba The Hutt's little sister you're almost there, girl.

Be confident

Guys are always attracted to girls who've got some self-love. Stand up straight, walk with pride and do what my mum says I never did enough of: smile.

Work your hair

It's a universal phenomenon that boys can't resist an onslaught of hair-flicking action. Short, long, straight, curly, red, blonde or brunette, they don't mind. So toss it, flip it, twist it, shake it all about.

Be your own style queen

As long as you're comfortable in your clothes, it doesn't matter what your look is. Some boys do have preferences but if yours is hippy, skatey, sporty or sexy it doesn't matter – as long as you have confidence he'll notice how great you look.

Crack him up

No boy has ever said, 'I really can't stand that girl, she always makes me laugh.' Even if your jokes are pathetic, a boy who likes you will laugh anyway.

Look interested

If it's got to the point where you're comfortable talking to him, then make it obvious you're interested in the stuff he's into, be it stamp-collecting or playing his guitar. This'll let him know you're keen, and he can make his move by asking you to check out his collection or catch his band rehearsal.

Be mysterious

I don't mean you should be Little Ms Flirt one day and a lady of mystery the next, but boys love a dash of intrigue, so keep him guessing about some parts of your life. In other words, don't stalk him and don't tell him how often you shave your armpits.

Be yourself

It sounds easy but this can be the hardest bit. He'll suss if you're faking who you are and what you're into. So be brave and just be your normal, sweet self. Well, that's the bit he's crazy about, isn't it?

THINGS THAT MAKE BOYS GO BLEURGH

Just as there are things that get boys going, there are things that make them go cold, so avoid:

- giggling uncontrollably;
- acting dumb;
- overdoing the make-up/hair gunge;
- mothering him;
- talking about other boys you fancy and/or ex-boyfriends;
- never having an opinion, and
- telling your mates all his secrets.

THE ASKING OUT BIT

You've had several chats, he's even walked you home a few times; you both like each other and you both know it. Aaargh, so when's he going to ASK YOU OUT?

You can do it

Boys love this method as it takes all the pressure off them. And even if you don't know him very well, he'll be flattered you fancy him.

So how do you do it? Keep the conversation

79

light and the pressure off. That way you'll be less nervous. Ask him casually if he fancies seeing a movie or going to the latest club night. If he doesn't respond immediately, don't get moody and upset – it can take a while for the penny to drop.

If he does turn you down, reply (as brightly as you can), 'Oh, don't worry, it's just a whole load of us are planning to go and I thought you'd like to go with us. See you later.' No one's the wiser (except you) and although you'll be gutted for a while at least you know so you can get over it.

On no account beg him, scream at him, cry in front of him or tell him he must be gay.

He can do it

Alternatively your crush boy may get round to asking you – eventually – although you may have to make the 'I fancy you' signs *soo* obvious that you've hired a billboard outside the school gates saying, 'Please ask me out, I won't say no.'

Whatever you do, don't interrupt him, don't ask him to speak up so all your mates can hear, don't roll your eyes, tut loudly and say, 'Finally . . .', and don't giggle.

Chapter 13

WHO'S YOUR PERFECT BOYFRIEND?

Ok, so you've been dreaming of your crush boy for, oh, a hundred years. But is he really the right one for you? Just because he looks ideal doesn't mean he's going to be an ideal boyfriend.

To find out whether your dream guy is a cheeky chappie or the strong, silent type try the quiz overleaf and identify your perfect boy:

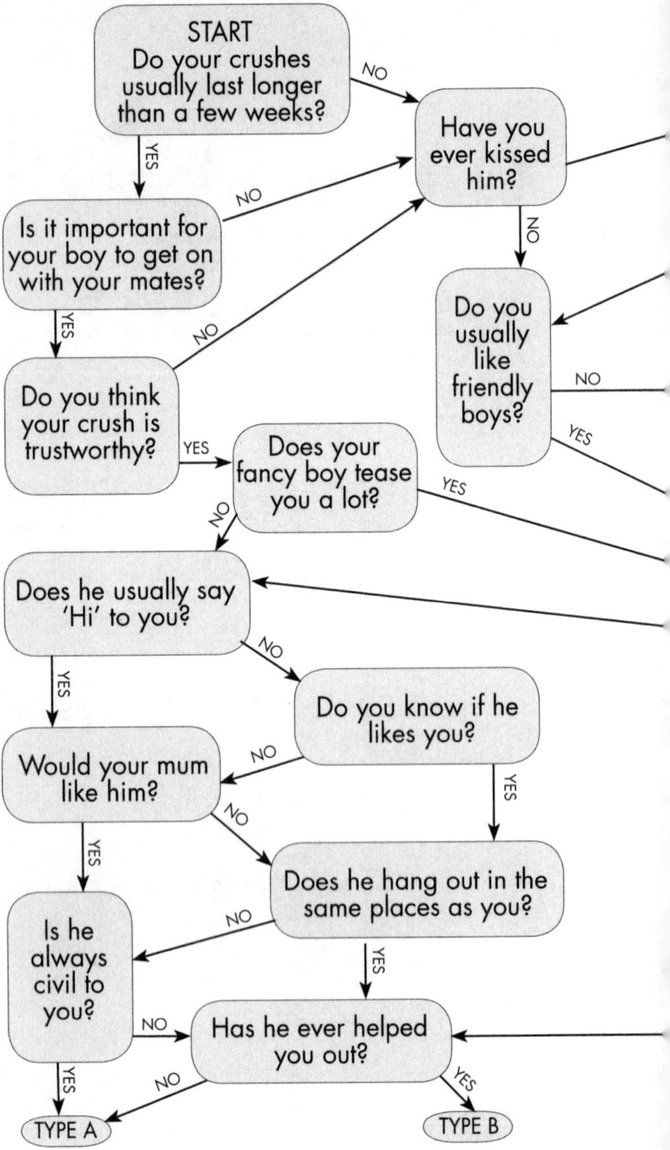

START
Do your crushes usually last longer than a few weeks?

NO →

YES ↓

Have you ever kissed him?

NO ↓

Is it important for your boy to get on with your mates?

NO →

YES ↓

Do you usually like friendly boys?

NO →

YES

Do you think your crush is trustworthy?

YES → Does your fancy boy tease you a lot?

NO

YES

Does he usually say 'Hi' to you?

NO →

YES ↓

Do you know if he likes you?

NO

YES ↓

Would your mum like him?

NO

YES ↓

Does he hang out in the same places as you?

NO

YES ↓

Is he always civil to you?

NO →

YES ↓

Has he ever helped you out?

YES → **TYPE B**

NO ↓

TYPE A

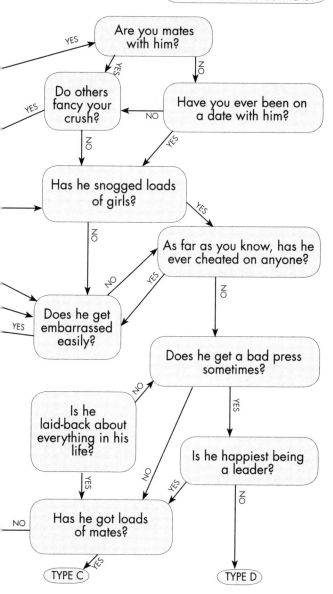

83

THE SMART GIRL'S GUIDE TO **BOYS**

Type A - Mr Quiet

You're attracted to the strong, silent type. He's full of passion and deep, brooding thoughts, but you'll need to put a rocket up his bum to get him to make the first move. If he's insecure about your feelings you'll have to work hard to make him relax and feel comfortable in your company. He's got old-fashioned notions of dating, so don't be surprised if he asks your folks if he can go out with you. Still, you'll always know where you stand with him.

Type B - Mr Cuddly

Your love destiny may be in the arms of a big softie. He's the dependable sort who likes to get on with things, which means making it obvious that you're the one for him. He'll make his intentions known by always popping up in the same places as you. You like a boy who you can treat as your best mate as well as your boyfriend and, being such a wise owl, he'll fulfil this desire tenfold. He loves to feel needed and will be totally devoted to you.

Type C – Mr Cheeky

You'd love your life to be as madcap as a Vic 'n' Bob comedy turn, and with this cheeky little monkey you're guaranteed never to have a dull moment. He's a born entertainer and he'll do anything to impress you too. He's full of energy and can be a hard one to pin down, but if he's got his heart set on you, he'll certainly use his dashing charm to captivate you. Watch out for his impulsive side because he's always full of surprises.

Type D – Mr Cool

He likes to cultivate the rebellious image, but behind this facade he's just as nervous as you. This boy has become an expert at hiding his true feelings behind a mask of indifference, but nothing could be further from the truth. He'll be a tough one to crack but once you do you'll be the object of his affection for a long time. He's loyal, truthful and 100% reliable. It's just that he's often misunderstood and finds it difficult to open up about himself.

Chapter 14

THE DATING GAME

You've got a date with the object of your lust, so now what are you going to do? If it's any consolation, he's as scared as you. Which is why I've devised this foolproof checklist, so hopefully all your dates will turn out great.

1 - Don't scare him

Chances are you've seen each other a billion times in school, hanging out, in yours/his daggy Saturday job uniforms, etc., so just wear something you're comfortable in and appropriate to where you're going. Oh, and before you leave the house check: body odour, bad breath, food in teeth, bogeys up nostrils and any signs of nervous farting.

2 - Compliment him

He's probably tried on (and sniffed) every item in his wardrobe/laundry basket and on his floor. Chances are, though, he'll still opt for the same trainers, jeans and shirt you've seen him in every day, but big difference: he or Mum has ironed his nifty togs. Put him at ease and say, 'You look great in that shirt, it's always been my favourite.'

3 - Meet somewhere neutral

It isn't a great idea to kick off your evening of cosy coupledom by subjecting him to the Spanish Inquisition Dad-stylee. If he has a car and you want him to pick you up, get him to meet you at the end of your street or alternatively make sure your folks are out. If neither of you have your own means of transport and don't relish the option of your folks ferrying you about all evening, pick a neutral meeting place that's easy for both of you to get to.

4 - Making plans

Boys are notoriously bad at asking you out, and worse still at deciding where to go on the date once they've finally asked you. For some strange reason, the 'what to do' bit always comes as a bit of a surprise – maybe they never count on you saying yes? Who knows, all I do know is it's probably up to you to come up with some plan of action. And whatever you do, make sure you can pay your way.

5 - Talk to him

Some boys are a bit slow at initiating conversations too, so this is another date dilemma you'll have to take the lead in. Don't witter on about your life story, but ask him leading questions about what he's into, like TV, footie, school, music, movies, computer games, etc. Remember, boys love to talk about anything *but* their feelings.

6 - Bumping into his mates

He'll spend all night worrying about this one. Even if you do bump into one of the most vulgar ones, smile sweetly, be friendly and pretend to ignore his mate's tales of their latest farting contest.

7 - Making a move

Again, you'll have to make your feelings pretty obvious. If he likes you and you start leaning closer to him, hopefully by the end of the evening he'll put his arm round you or hold your hand.

8 – The kissing stuff

So you've both sussed out you like each other. By the end of the date you'll both have the same thoughts running through your mind: Should I lean in closer? Is he shy? Is she shy? Does he think I'm revolting? Does she think I'm ugly? Should I kiss her on the mouth or cheek? and so on.

If you want to snog him (and you're confident he wants to snog you back), you could say, 'I've really enjoyed myself tonight. Thank you.' Then give him a big hug and look straight into his eyes. Most boys would respond to this sign of encouragement.

If he's more of a dibbo than a dreamboat, then thank him all the same, but do this *after* he's got you home safely, as you head inside quickly with a cheery 'Bye-bye'.

The perfect kiss: If your boy's a novice kisser, he'll probably lunge in and make a right mess of it. Don't despair and don't worry if you're a beginner too. The key to super-snogging is to take your time and you'll learn instinctively to know what you both like. Here are a few handy tips:

1 Place your slightly-opened mouth lightly against his. You can keep your eyes closed so you don't feel so self-conscious.

2 Move your mouth, slightly closing and opening it, moving it slowly and rhythmically in sync with his.

3 Gently suck his lips with yours as you kiss.

4 If you fancy it, this is now the perfect time to use your tongue. Slip yours into his mouth for a second. If he doesn't spit it out in horror, but starts using his too, this is when you can both explore each other's mouths. You're now officially French kissing.

5 So that you don't make like a washing machine, slow down the speed and pressure of your snogging. Use gentle pecks, nuzzle his neck and earlobes or nibble or suck his lower lip.

6 Finish off with a slow, tender sucking on his lower lip.

What happens to the hands?': Don't keep them clamped to your sides, or he'll think you're weird. Cuddle him by placing one arm round his waist and the other over his shoulder, or even wrap both arms round his shoulders or neck – whatever you feel comfortable with. As for him, if he's gagging for a quick grope, tell him where to get off and make it clear he's only got snogging privileges at the moment. If he really likes you, he'll lay off.

9 – The 'What now?' bit

Boys are pathetic at saying goodbye, no matter how they feel about you. They have no idea what to say if they want to see you again. They're petrified of looking too keen and scaring you off, but equally they don't want to hurt your feelings if they'd rather not go on a second date. So invariably you'll get a mumbled, 'Er, I'll call you soon. OK?' or 'See you, then,' no matter what he's thinking about you.

10 – The phone call

Boys are terrible phone phobics. So don't spend your precious time waiting for him to call. If he likes you he will – eventually. After your first date it's best not to assume anything, especially 'We've been on a date, we've kissed, so we must be boyfriend and girlfriend.' Ultimately, if you've had a good time, then he probably has too. He just has to play it as cool as possible for at least the first couple of weeks. Of course, you could call, text message or e-mail him but generally boys in their misguided machoness will like to take the lead. But letting him know you're still interested is no bad thing, and at least you'll know where you stand and can put yourself out of that will-he-won't-he-call-me? agony.

Some boys take phone numbers just for fun or out of politeness. Of course the chief reason a boy doesn't call is probably because he's realised he's not into you as much as he thought. But don't blame yourself if he doesn't call. Don't start thinking 'I'm so ugly, no one'll ever want to go out with me,' because that's utter rubbish.

And what if he does call and he's not *the* one? Give him the brush-off gently: say you're spending most weekends away with your cousins, looking after a sick aunty or snowed under with heaps of schoolwork. He'll get the hint.

And what if *the* one calls? Don't squeal down the receiver as he's asking you what you're up to next weekend. Keep as calm as poss, say, 'Oh, hang on a min' (pretend to check your diary), return to the phone, and say, 'Yeah, Saturday's fine, how about a movie or bowling?'

Ooh, get you! This could be the start of a beautiful relationship!

Chapter 15

BOY BLUNDERS TO AVOID

When you're mad about your hornbud, and you'd rather like your relationship to last longer than a couple of weeks, you've got to play it super-smart. It's all too easy to get carried away with your feelings and take your relationship too far too soon.

Sin 1 – Hero worship

Everyone likes to feel special, but there's a big difference between showing your boy how much you care about him and sanctifying an altar to him in the corner of your bedroom. Boys freak out if a girl dedicates her entire life to them.

Kate, 18, from Buckinghamshire, remembers: 'I was so crazy about my first boyfriend, Russell, that

I single-handedly pushed him and all my mates away by my non-stop "Russell likes this, Russell does this" chat. I ditched my friends whenever he called, but when we were together I'd put him so high on a pedestal I'd become a pathetic airhead gazing adoringly into his face. How shameful. He soon ditched me for a girl with a mind of her own.'

Your salvation: Don't make him the centre of your universe. No boy can fulfil your every social and emotional need. Hold on to your own friend-ships and interests.

Sin 2 – Keeping him from his friends

If you're mad about a boy it's only natural you want to spend practically every waking moment with him. But if he wants to hang out with his mates don't get offended, and don't put the pressure on. The harder you try to pull him away from his mates, the higher the odds he'll pull away from you. And don't be surprised if he acts differently when his mates are around – the chances are that you're different with your mates. It's natural and doesn't mean he's shallow or insincere.

Your salvation: How would you feel if he pres-surised you to stop seeing your mates? It doesn't

matter what you think of his friends, he likes them
so you'll just have to learn how to share him fairly.

Sin 3 – Getting jealous of other girls

OK, so if he's always flirting with that drop-dead
gorgeous sixth former or an ex-girlfriend, then it's
pretty normal to feel well narked and jealous. But
if you're experiencing the green-eyed paranoia
even when he asks the lollipop lady for the time,
you've got problems.

Your salvation: You have to get a handle on
your insecurity: build up your self-esteem and drop
the possessive behaviour. After all, he's going out
with you, isn't he?

Sin 4 - Trying to change him

If he insists on wearing tartan shorts and striped
shirts, then a little gentle persuasion and a quick
shopping trip supervised by you is perfectly justi-
fied. But he's going to start wondering if you're his
mum in disguise if you insist on changing everything from his hairstyle to his CD collection.

Your salvation: There must've been something
about him which made you fancy him in the first
place. Try to remember this when you're frog-

marching him to the nearest barbers, otherwise he'll soon be hopping out of your life.

Sin 5 – Going too far too soon

Boys feel honour-bound to push their luck in the saucy stakes. However the majority of them don't expect to get too far too soon, so don't ever feel pressured into doing anything intimate unless you've seriously considered all the consequences, are using condoms, and you're ready and willing. It's a massive mistake to think a bit of horizontal jogging will **a** make him love you forever, **b** stop him from dumping you or **c** work if he's promised you **a** and **b**.

Natasha, 17, from Cardiff, remembers her first time: 'I believed doing "it" with Michael would make him commit to me. It didn't, and to give him his due he never promised it would. But I was heartbroken when he broke up with me, mainly because we'd been so intimate.'

Your salvation: Don't ever give in to pressure. Any boy who seriously cares will back off if you tell him you're not ready, and respect your decision. But a boy who keeps pestering you is better off being given the big push himself.

Chapter 16

ARE YOU A HEAVENLY MATCH?

Any girl who hasn't made it her business to discover her fancy guy's star sign is ignoring some vital info for unlocking his heart . . .

Aries: 21 March – 20 April
What's he like?: He's energetic, loud and very confident. This boy has a real ambitious streak and will use his popularity and charm to get whatever he wants. Don't be timid. Aries boys love girls with attitude, and none of them can resist a challenge. Speak up with your own opinions and you'll get him doing a double-take.
Watch out for: He's a cheeky chappie with a bossy nature, and a terrible loser too.
Compatible with: Gemini, Leo, Sagittarius.

THE SMART GIRL'S GUIDE TO **BOYS**

Taurus: 21 April – 21 May

What's he like?: He can be a tough cookie to crack, but once he's crumbled under your wily ways he's a genuine softie. He's a great listener and very trustworthy. Give him loads of encouragement, er, like talking to him, all the while 'accidentally' touching his arm as you're doing it. He's not that confident so you'll have to be brave, take the initiative and be obvious.

Watch out for: He's stubborn and insecure, with a temper and a jealous streak.

Compatible with: Cancer, Virgo, Capricorn.

Gemini: 22 May – 21 June

What's he like?: This boy really, really likes to talk. He's the nosey-parker of the zodiac and one of the most sociable and fun too. He can act like a hyperactive toddler but at least there's never a dull moment with him. Make him laugh or ideally laugh heartily at his pranks.

Watch out for: He's forgetful and tactless at times. He also worries far too much about what others think of him.

Compatible with: Leo, Libra, Aquarius.

Cancer: 22 June – 22 July

What's he like?: Cautious, fussy but very sincere are his characteristics. Because he's happy pottering around in his own little world, this is sometimes seen as shyness, but he's a master at hiding his true feelings. You'll need to befriend him first, then dazzle him with your intelligent conversation. You'll get a better result if you're not surrounded by all your mates – he's more relaxed on his own.

Watch out for: He's a high-maintenance guy who needs loads of attention. Plus he's terrible for holding grudges – and never forgives or forgets.

Compatible with: Virgo, Scorpio, Pisces.

Leo: 23 July – 23 Aug.

What's he like?: Practically every Leo is a total charmer and loves to have fun. He's popular and a bit of a cheeky monkey. You can rely on him to be a true peacemaker though – he hates arguments. He admires girls with a mind of their own, and no Leo can resist a compliment.

Watch out for: Leos like their own space (in which to shine), and this can lead to periods of self-centredness and egotistical tendencies.

Compatible with: Libra, Sagittarius, Aries.

Virgo: 24 Aug. - 23 Sept.

What's he like?: He's analytical, smart and resourceful. This guy loves to have a good think, and he will rarely do anything without weighing up the pros and cons of his actions. He's very funny and he notices everything. Ask him something specific; Virgos are sticklers for detail, and he'll love that quality in you. He's a boy who loves having an ego boost, so tell him how great he is.

Watch out for: His sensitive and silent moody side. He'll go into a grump at any criticism, how-ever minor.

Compatible with: Scorpio, Capricorn, Taurus.

Libra: 24 Sept. - 23 Oct.

What's he like?: One of the zodiac's true diplo-mats. He hates to see any unfairness, and will do anything for a harmonious life. This doesn't mean to say he can't be cheeky too, but he'll always talk his way out of trouble. Play up to his visual side: Libras love anyone who shows their own sense of style. They are also partial to girls who'll take the initiative, as it takes the pressure off them to make the move.

Watch out for: Indecision. He likes to chill out, and hates to feel under pressure to make any decision. At their worst, Libras can be too superficial.
Compatible with: Sagittarius, Aquarius, Gemini.

Scorpio: 24 Oct. – 22 Nov.

What's he like?: Passionate and full of action, this guy can't sit still for a second. The problem is he's very selective about who he hangs out with. He's a secretive person but witty, and very intelligent. Scorpios love some mystery so you'll need to use a huge dose of hypnotic charm to match his.
Watch out for: His perceptive nature means it's easy for him to toy with others' emotions. He can be cruel and loves playing games.
Compatible with: Capricorn, Pisces, Cancer.

Sagittarius: 23 Nov. – 21 Dec.

What's he like?: A real laugh. This boy can't help but find himself the centre of attention. His loud facade hides a really generous soul. He'll do anything for his mates. Be spontaneous: Sagittarians love surprises and love girls who know how to have a good time. These boys are daring, so they need little encouragement to strike up a conversation.

101

Watch out for: He's the flirtmeister of the zodiac and loves to charm every girl he meets. Saggies are restless boys and can lack staying power.

Compatible with: Aquarius, Aries, Leo.

Capricorn: 22 Dec. – 20 Jan.

What he's like?: He's dependable and loyal, but he's got a mind of his own too, and will crack everyone up with his wacky sense of humour. He can appear aloof at times but he's sensitive and a true sweetheart. These boys are cautious in the extreme. You'll need to walk up to him with a billboard emblazoned 'I fancy you' before he'll be 100% sure you're not going to reject him.

Watch out for: Predictability and boredom. He resents anything new popping up without warning in his world and can be quite pig-headed too.

Compatible with: Pisces, Taurus, Virgo.

Aquarius: 21 Jan. – 19 Feb.

What's he like?: This boy is a total individual, with a unique sense of humour and his own unique viewpoints too. He can appear aloof and detached but he's really busy daydreaming. Anything that makes you stand out from the crowd will ensure you'll get noticed by him. He admires quirkiness, the weirder the better. Play up to his sense of fun and need for stimulating chat and he's yours.

Watch out for: His contrary ways. He can change his mind more times than he changes his pants.

Compatible with: Aries, Gemini, Libra.

Pisces: 20 Feb. – 20 March

What's he like?: He's very intuitive and sensitive to the needs of others. Don't be fooled by his calm, dreamy exterior though, because he's ambitious and doesn't let others push him around. Be creative. If you're a whizz at art, poetry, drama or music you're halfway there. Pisces boys love a girl with a passion, so show him how committed you can be, whether it's netball or saving the baby seals.

Watch out for: His wild mood swings. Pisces believe they're guardians of morality and are easily offended.

Compatible with: Taurus, Cancer, Scorpio.

Chapter 17

IS HE FALLING FOR YOU?

It doesn't matter if you've been on one date or 374 with your boy, this whole dating game is a confusing merry-go-round of emotions. You're pretty certain you're falling for him big-time, but is he thinking the same about you? Don't get stressed: you need to get smart on the tell-tale boy signs that shout out, 'I'm crazy for you!'

He performs random acts of kindness

Does he automatically plump up the sofa cushions for you before settling down to watch a vid? Has he reorganised your CD collection in chronological and alphabetical order? If your boy's performed any of the above without you asking, you're on to a winner. He's gagging to take care of you and this is his sweet way of showing you.

He does things he hates

So you're desperate to see *The Beach* for the hundredth time, only problem is your guy hates Leo. But if your boy agrees to chaperone you to the local fleapit to keep you happy, you've got him hooked. Boys will only risk public humiliation and personal boredom in the name of love. This applies to shopping, too. Only boys who are potty about their sweetheart will follow her around Top Shop on a Saturday afternoon.

He makes you do stuff you hate

When he digs his treasured footie sticker albums out from the bottom of his wardrobe to show you, or whisks you off to the local skateboard shop, you can bet he's ballistic about you.

He spends less time with his mates

It's an unspoken sign with boys, but if yours is head over heels for you, his mates'll have to start putting up Missing In Action posters around town.

Boys who are into their girlfriends will naturally want to spend most of their spare time with her and not their mates.

He teases you

Does he think it's hilarious when he's taking the mick out of the way you say, 'Shut up!'? Does he tease you about your hair serum collection? If he's into teasing and acting in an odd goofball way too, he's majorly loved-up. Boys have to feel very happy and secure before they show you their nutty side.

He's introduced you to his parents

This is major-league in the love stakes. No boy in his right mind would risk this kind of embarrassment unless you meant a lot to him. He's making a statement that you're the most important person in his life, and he wants the other VIPs in his life to know you too. (Regardless of the baby pics you'll see that'll make him cringe.)

He tells you everything

If your boy's confiding the most squirm-filled moments of his life to you, he's falling for you badly. Opening up to a girl is a high-risk factor for any guy, and for him to do so means he trusts you not to spill his secrets to your mates, or laugh heartily at his fears, worries and hopes. The more personal the info he shares, the closer he's feeling to you.

He argues with you

I'm not talking about the 'bad' kind of arguing, where a boy'll pick on something you've said just to put you down or to take out his bad mood on you, but 'good', 'interesting' arguments. Yes, they do exist! If your boy's picking your brain on how you feel about issues, it's a sure sign he's trying to find out where you're coming from so you can both make the relationship work. It's called having a 'frank and honest exchange of opinions'.

He understands you

It's that time of the month when he can do nothing right, and you're screaming how much you hate him. He'll smile sweetly and say, 'Yes, dear'. Whether you have rows when you're pre-menstrual or not makes no difference – he'll say sorry if he's in the wrong and wait for you to apologise if you've been naughty.

He brags about you

If your boy's friends are congratulating you on your good grades or winning the school title for champion goalshooter, it's obvious he can't help telling anyone who'll listen what a top girl you are.

He talks to you every day

Boys love to act cool, but when he's falling for you, cool isn't an option in his rule book. Not all couples (however much they care) feel the need to see each other every single day, but if he's diving into your pool of love, he'll feel the urge to talk to you at least once a day.

He discusses future plans

If he's making plans about what the two of you'll do over the summer holidays, or how you'll celebrate New Year's Eve, this boy is sending some very clear commitment messages. Generally guys in their quest to look cool and spontaneous will avoid any attempts to be pinned down about what they're up to Friday night let alone three months down the line. So if yours is actively planning your future together – he's seriously smitten.

Chapter 18

YOU AND THE SEX STUFF

If you and your boy are getting serious about each other, the chances are there'll come a point in your relationship when you'll have to get serious about the issue of sex.

Relationships are full of various degrees of intimacy, both emotionally and physically, so the question you have to ask yourself is whether you are ready to take your relationship to a level of sexual intimacy. This is when you need to take time out with your boy and both of you will need to discuss what's going on, and where you want to take it.

It isn't easy being sensible about sex (even people who've been at it for years make awful mistakes) but it's absolutely vital, both emotionally and physically, for you to realise what a minefield the whole business can be. Don't ever feel pressured to have sex – this is the ultimate recipe for disaster. It's easy to feel pressurised: you could be experiencing pressure from your boyfriend, your mates, or you could even be putting pressure on yourself, thinking sex will transform you into a 'woman'! Don't give in to any of these – ever! It's your body and your life, and only you will truly know when the time is right.

Crap lines boys'll say to get your knickers off

Sometimes, when the urge is on them, boys will say anything to try to get their wicked way – stooping to emotional blackmail and all kinds of dubious logic. No smart girl should ever fall for any of these . . .

- 'But I really love you.'
- 'It'll prove how much we love each other.'
- 'If you don't I know someone who will.'
- 'I can't wait forever.'
- 'But my balls will turn blue.'
- 'I just want to hold you.'
- 'It'll prove you're not frigid.'

Don't be fooled – and if he can stoop that low,
you may want to ask yourself if you can like and
respect someone who'll act like that . . .

The ultimate sex checklist

Before you do anything, answer yes or no to the
following questions:

1 Can you talk about sex without
getting the giggles? Y ☐ N ☐

2 Do you honestly believe you and
your boy are in love? Y ☐ N ☐

3 Have you ever discussed
contraception with your boy? Y ☐ N ☐

4 Do you trust your boy 100%? Y ☐ N ☐

5 Are you listening to your head? Y ☐ N ☐

6 Do you know how you can catch
chlamydia, herpes or AIDs? Y ☐ N ☐

7 Are most of your mates bragging
about sex, and do you feel left out? Y ☐ N ☐

8 Do you believe sex will make you
a woman? Y ☐ N ☐

9 Do you think you love each other? Y ☐ N ☐

10 Do you believe it'll prove he
loves you? Y ☐ N ☐

• If you answered **yes** to most of the questions **1** to **6** you're well on your way to dealing with intimacy in a very mature and responsible manner. If you do decide to go ahead and have sex, make sure you always use a condom.

• If you answered **yes** to most of the questions **7** to **10** you need to slow down and reassess why you're so keen to get horizontal with your boy. At the moment you're thinking of doing it for all the wrong reasons.

• If you answered **no** to most of the questions **1** to **6** you're heading for big emotional – and physical – problems. On no account believe any suggestions that you're ready for a sexual relationship because you're clearly not.

• If you answered **no** to most of the questions **7** to **10** you've got your head screwed on the right way and are not fooled by others or likely to cave in to pressure. You're confident and sensible and will trust your own instincts.

SEX MATTERS

Everyone knows the law which states that having sex with a girl who's under the age of sixteen is illegal. It's there for a reason – to protect you,

mentally, emotionally and physically.

In Britain, the average age for losing your virginity is seventeen. So if all your mates are claiming to be sexperts, the chances are they're telling porkies. But only you can tell if you're truly ready, willing and able to jump aboard the emotional rollercoaster that having sex will take you on. So next time you're in serious danger of getting carried away as the passion rating rises, go through the ultimate sex checklist in your head, and if you have any doubts, then stop!

One thing's guaranteed: if you haven't got the confidence to tell him to stop, then you're lacking the maturity to let him into your knickers. If you're worried, uncomfortable or have any niggling doubts, say so as clearly as possible and don't ever think you have to apologise for not wanting sex.

Be prepared

If you are going to have sex with your boyfriend, the best thing you can both do is to be prepared. Work out where and when you're going to do it, so you can make the whole experience as special and as memorable as you possibly can.

One essential preparation is to *talk* to your

boyfriend about how you both feel, and what you both expect to gain from the whole experience. Only by talking, talking and talking some more will you both be able to relax about the whole situation, and even laugh about things. And another essential point: get professional advice on contraception. Also talk with your boyfriend about it and make sure he uses condoms so you're protected against unwanted pregnancy and STIs, especially the HIV virus, which can lead to AIDS.

Losing your virginity

This has to be something you want to do, on your own terms. Having sex for the first time is something you will remember for the rest of your life. So be nice to yourself and make it as good as it can possibly be. The last thing you want to do is to remember your first time full of regret. Having sex usually takes your relationship on to another level of intimacy and commitment. Which is why it's vital that, hand on heart, you honestly believe he's the right one, and the one boy you want to lose your virginity to – not just a boy you're lusting after this month.

The first time

Don't expect too much from your first time. It's not likely to be a rerun of what you've seen in the movies. Life's rarely like that! The two of you will need to be realistic and try to keep your sense of humour.

Sex is an intimate business which means it can be both embarrassing and messy too. It can also hurt a little, so take it easy and don't do anything you feel uncomfortable about. The two of you may fumble about, trying to put the condom on, and as for orgasms – don't expect one the first time round! Just try and relax and don't feel disappointed if it doesn't live up to your expectations. Neither you nor he will be a sexpert the first time round, and don't be horrified if you, he or you both make strange, embarrassing noises: things like farting, burping, 'fanny' farts and tummy rumblings can and may happen. So chill out and whether it lasts ten seconds, ten minutes or half an hour, just do what comes naturally and don't feel pressured to do anything against your will.

Be true to yourself

If you regret having sex, you don't have to spend the next ten years regretting your decision. Losing your virginity is usually a bigger deal for girls than it is for most boys, and if you do regret losing your virginity, don't despair and think you've ruined everything. OK, you'll never be a virgin again, but just because you've done it once doesn't mean you have to keep on doing it. There's no law saying you have to keep on having sex with the same person just because you've done it with him already. And you don't have to have sex with your next boyfriend, just because you've done it with one before. You're in control and it's your decision when you have sex again.

CONTRACEPTION

Never even think about having sex without first having considered contraception, which is the only way to protect yourself against unwanted pregnancy. Regardless of how well you know and trust your partner you also need to protect yourself against sexually transmitted infections (STIs), which are discussed starting on page 122. The male and female condoms are the only contraceptives that give both contraception and STI protection. So if you use another kind of contraceptive, you must always use a condom as well. Always be safe. Always use a condom!

It is usually best to get advice on contraception from a doctor or family planning clinic. These are the different contraceptive options available:

Condom

A thin latex sheath that covers the erect penis. It catches the sperm rather than letting it go inside you.

Effectiveness: 85 – 98% effective.

Pros: It's free from family planning clinics and can be bought in any chemist or pub/bar and restaurant toilets.

Cons: It can slip off or tear if not used properly.

Remember: Use a new condom each time. Make sure the packet has a British Kitemark or European CE mark on it and check the expiry date.

STI protection?: YES.

Female condom

A thin polyurethane sleeve that fits into the vagina. It blocks the sperm from going into your cervix.

Effectiveness: 85- 98% effective.

Pros: It can be put in any time before sex.

Cons: It can be tricky to use and expensive.

Remember: You have to fit a new one each time you have sex.

STI protection?: YES.

The pill

There are two types of contraceptive pill – the combined pill (a mixture of the hormones oestrogen and progestogen, which stops you producing an egg each month) and the progestogen-only pill (which thickens cervical mucus, making it hard for the sperm to swim up the Fallopian tubes. It also thins the womb lining, making it inhospitable for a fertilised egg). To get a prescription you must see your doctor, who'll advise on the best type for you.

Effectiveness: The combined pill is virtually 100% safe. The progestogen-only pill is 96–99% safe.

Pros: The combined pill reduces bleeding, period pain and PMS. It can also protect against cancer in the ovary or womb.

Cons: On the combined pill, you can get some side-effects like headaches and feeling sick, bloating and weight gain. On the progestogen-only pill your periods may become irregular, with some bleeding in between.

Remember: It's not suitable for everyone – your

doctor will advise. You take the pills daily, and you must take the progestogen-only pill at the same time every day.

STI protection?: NO.

Diaphragm or cap

It's a soft rubber disk or bowl that fits at the top of your vagina and covers your cervix. Used with a spermicide, it stops sperm entering your cervix.

Effectiveness: 85-96%.

Pros: It can be put in a few hours before sex.

Cons: If you have sex a second time, you need to use more spermicide. It can be tricky to learn how to use the cap, and you have to leave it in for hours after you have had sex.

Remember: You have to get it fitted by your doctor.

STI protection?: NO.

Contraceptive injection

Depro Provera is an injection of the hormone pro-gestogen. It disrupts your production of eggs and your menstrual cycle.

Effectiveness: 99%.

Pros: After the injection you are protected

from conception for twelve weeks.

Cons: You can get some side-effects like irregular periods and weight gain.

Remember: Once you've had one, you can't stop it until it runs out.

STI protection?: NO.

Contraceptive implant

It's a hormone capsule which is surgically inserted into your arm. The hormone is time-released and stops you ovulating. It also thickens the mucus in your cervix, helping stop sperm reaching the egg.

How effective: 99%.

Pros: It works for five years, so you needn't worry about contraception.

Cons: It's hard to have it removed if you change your mind. It can also cause periods to become irregular and you can get side-effects like greasy hair and acne.

Remember: Once it's in, you can't see it.

STI protection?: NO.

The IUS

This is the Intra Uterine System. It's a small, T-shaped plastic device which contains the hormone progestogen. It slowly releases the progestogen, which thickens the mucus in your cervix, helping to stop sperm reaching an egg, and it thins the womb lining, making it inhospitable to an egg. It is fitted into your womb by a doctor.

Effectiveness: Almost 100%.

Pros: It works for at least three years and periods can get shorter and lighter.

Cons: You might get irregular bleeding and have side-effects like tender boobs and acne.

Remember: You feel it's in place by some light threads which hang into your vagina.

STI protection?: NO.

The IUD

Similar to the IUS, this is the Intra Uterine Device. It's a small plastic and copper device, usually shaped like a 'T', that is fitted into the uterus by a doctor. It stops sperm meeting an egg, or stops an egg settling in the womb.

Effectiveness: 98-99%.

Pros: It works for five years.

Cons: You may get heavier and more painful periods.

Remember: It is unsuitable for women who

have more than one sexual partner. It's not often given to young women.

STI protection?: NO.

All information taken from the Family Planning Clinic's leaflet Is Everybody Doing It? Your Guide To Contraception.

SEXUALLY TRANSMITTED INFECTIONS

It's not only contraception you need to know about. Unfortunately you'll need to be aware of all the diseases you're at risk of catching. Be aware that many of these sexually-transmitted infections do not produce physical symptoms for many months, which means you may catch them from someone who has no symptoms, and you also risk infecting others through unprotected sex. Always be safe. Always use a condom! If you think you may have an infection, consult a doctor for advice and treatment where applicable.

Chlamydia
One of the most common STIs in the UK. Women aged sixteen to nineteen are most at risk. If not

treated it can lead to infertility. It is passed through vaginal sex, or by transferring the infection from his or your genitals to the eyes by touching genitals and then touching the eyes.

Symptoms: Most women don't have any symptoms. But you should watch out for: a mild increase in vaginal discharge, the need to wee more often and painful weeing, stomach ache and irregular bleeding, pain during sex, swelling or eye irritation.

The cure: Antibiotics.

Genital herpes

There are two different types of this virus: type I causes sores on the nose and mouth and type II causes sores in the genital and anal area. It's passed through direct contact with an infected person, through kissing, oral, vaginal or anal sex. You can catch herpes from someone who may have no signs of it all.

Symptoms: You'll get an itching or tingling sensation around the mouth or genital/anal area. Small blisters then develop, which burst and leave painful sores. You might also get flu-like symptoms. During this period the virus is highly infectious and so all sexual contact should be avoided.

The cure: NONE. Once you catch it, you can't cure it – but you have to learn to live with it. Attacks can reoccur at any time.

Genital warts

They are small fleshy growths, like tiny cauliflowers, that grow on or around the genital area/anus. They're transmitted through skin to skin contact of the genitals, in vaginal, anal and oral sex. They can cause cancer in women, and are best treated immediately on discovery.

Symptoms: Some strains of the virus can be almost invisible, others look like the description above. They may itch, but usually they are painless.

The cure: Podophyllin, a paint-on solution, is often used, or they can be frozen off or laser treated.

Gonorrhoea

This is also known as 'the clap'. It's a bacterial infection caught through vaginal, anal or oral sex.

Symptoms: Women may not show any symptoms. However weeing may become painful, and a sore throat can develop. If left untreated, a rash can develop that can affect the nervous system.

The cure: Penicillin.

HIV and AIDS

HIV is Human Immunodeficiency Virus. An infected person is HIV Positive. HIV attacks the body's immune system. People with HIV usually stay well for many years before they develop AIDS itself. AIDS stands for Acquired Immune Deficiency Syndrome. It is also a collection of illnesses and conditions that arise as the body's immune system is weakened by HIV infection. HIV is transmitted through unprotected sex, including anal sex. The highly infectious virus can't survive outside the body, but it is passed through bodily fluids like semen or vaginal secretions. This means that unprotected oral sex is a risk if there are cuts or lesions present.

Symptoms: HIV symptoms are: night sweats, fever, lack of energy, diarrhoea and weight-loss, thrush or herpes infections, dry skin and rashes, mouth ulcers and bleeding gums. AIDS-related symptoms which can develop are: breathing problems, eyesight difficulties and infections, brain problems and cancer.

The cure: NONE.

Hepatitis

A viral infection of the liver. Hepatitis A is not a sexually transmitted infection. However, Hepatitis B is more infectious than HIV and can be spread through sexual contact, and contact with blood or saliva containing blood traces.

Symptoms: Lack of energy, appetite, fever, jaundiced (yellow) skin, yellowing of the whites of the eyes, pale poo and dark wee and abdominal pain.

The cure: NONE. But some do recover after rest and adopting a healthy lifestyle.

OTHER INFECTIONS

There are a few infections women may develop, but these aren't usually sexually transmitted and are easily treatable:

Thrush

Thrush is a result of a bacterial imbalance of a fungus naturally occuring in the vagina. It can be triggered by stress, taking antibiotics, wearing tight-fitting clothes or sex with someone who has thrush. Symptoms can include: vaginal soreness and inflammation and/or pain when weeing.

Some may notice an increase in vaginal discharge, which has changed colour, smells and itches.

The cure: Creams available from chemists. Sex should be avoided until it has cleared up.

Cystitis

An infection/inflammation of the bladder lining, which makes it very painful to wee. It also makes you think you want to wee all the time. Usually it's a consequence of sexual intercourse or of not drinking enough fluids. Wearing tight trousers or knickers can also cause bacteria to breed.

The cure: Drink half a litre of water immediately when symptoms develop and then a quarter of a litre every 20 minutes until you wee without any pain. Don't resist the urge to wee, as any urine passed will help to flush out the infection. There are also various treatments available from the chemist.

PREGNANCY

If you're using condoms and/or other contraception, the chances are you won't get pregnant. However accidents do happen, so what are your choices if you find out you're pregnant?

127

Firstly you must get help and advice. Talk to a trusted adult, your boyfriend, your doctor, a school nurse, teacher and your parents. Don't be scared about telling your mum and dad: they may not like your news but 99.9% of parents will help and support you through what will be the most difficult time of your life. You'll need all the support you can get in helping you make the right decision.

Basically you have three options: You can keep the baby, you can have the baby adopted or you can have an abortion.

Whatever one you opt for, each one has far-reaching consequences for your life, both emotionally, physically and even financially. So please don't tackle this dilemma on your own. Don't ignore the problem: get help immediately.

STRESSED ABOUT SEX?

If you've got any questions about sex, you'll find help at the following:

The Family Planning Association
Contraceptive Helpline: 020 7837 4044
(Mon–Fri 9 a.m. – 7 p.m.) for your nearest clinic.
Brook Advisory Centres: free helpline on 0800 0185 023
(Mon, Tues, Thurs 9 a.m.– 5 p.m.
Wed & Fri 9 a.m. – 4 p.m.) for your local branch.
ChildLine: free 24-hour helpline on 0800 1111.
National AIDS Helpline: free 24-hour helpline on 0800 567123.

Chapter 19

DEALING WITH A BREAK-UP

So you've got together with the boy of your dreams. But suddenly things don't seem so wonderful. Getting to know a boy can be great – but there are some boys that you begin to feel you'd rather not spend your precious time with . . .

BOYS WHO BELONG IN THE BIN

The incurable flirt

He'll sweep you off your feet, but this one can't stop playing games with your heart. He constantly needs attention (from other girls) and revels in his charming ways. If you're looking for a short-term affair, he's the one but monogamy and commitment are not in his vocabulary.

The cheat

He's the incurable flirt who can't say no. There is no excuse for wasting your time on a boyfriend who is cheating or has cheated on you. He's sacrificed the trust between you and deserves nothing from you but a big 'goodbye'.

The emotional cripple

You can't pinpoint anything specific, but he never makes you feel comfortable and relaxed. You'd love to reveal your feelings or how an exam is really stressing you out, but you can't talk to him. If you can't be yourself with him, who are you going to be?

The personality basher

Does he criticise your clothes? Or say your hair looks a mess? Does he pressure you for sex? Is rude about your family and friends? Has a real mood-on if you're not paying him enough attention? This one makes out he's doing you a favour by going out with you. Don't waste your energy wondering how you're ever going to please him: be nice to yourself and get rid of him – fast.

The blagger

He's only interested in what he can get out of you, i.e.: your homework, or access to your mates/Dreamcast/Sky TV. You should only go out with boys who are interested in you, not your material possessions.

The slacker

He's always got time for you and will always be loads of fun, but he'll never be able to pay his way and he'll never make any effort for you – or even for himself. If all you want is to kick back and forget your responsibilities, he's your boy.

The bad boy

He's a real-life rebel without a cause: skipping school, failing exams, picking fights and generally making a right mess of his life. He's exciting to be with for, oh, about three days but he's his own worst enemy, so don't think you're going to change him. Only he can do that, and he won't necessarily realise he's messed up until it's way too late.

The one with a girlfriend

Don't ever fall into a love triangle: it's not a clever

place to be in. The only one who loses out will be you. You'll never be able to go out in public with him, you'll only see him on his terms, and if he did bin his girl for you, could you trust him completely? What's to stop him from cheating on you? . . .

The ex-boyfriend

Going out with your ex is like chomping on a Mars Bar: you know exactly what to expect. He's never going to change his annoying habits and you're never going to be something you're not. Stay mates and hang out together, but don't believe the second time round will be any better, because it won't be.

Your ex's friend/your friend's ex

If you want to run the risk of losing your best mate or indeed any of your mates, then go out with their exes. Also dating any of your ex's friends is liable to cause major friction and hurt feelings with your ex. Respect his territory and go sharking in fresher waters.

THE TOP NINE BREAKING-UP STRATEGIES

If it's not working, and your relationship is more stress than fun, then it's probably time to bail out. But often this can be the most difficult and painful thing to do. Here are the most commonly-used methods for dumping a boyfriend.

A cruel break: The hide & seek method

This is the action-speaks-louder-than-words strategy. But what if he's not listening? Avoiding him and his calls may seem the easiest and least painful option – for you – but isn't an easy option when he turns up on your doorstep to ask you what the problem is. If you opt for this one, you might have to move in with your best mate for two months, and change your mobile number too.

A bad break: The flirt's method

Begging your best boy mate to pretend he's your new boyfriend, or flirting with every guy in full view of the-one-you're-trying-to-dump isn't a very nice way of telling him it's over. If you have any affection left for him try not to be so heartless.

A naughty break: The phone method

This can be easier, and extremely practical, if you're having a long-distance relationship, but not so good if he's the boy-next-door. You don't have to explain yourself face to face but there's a high probability he'll hang up on you. Just don't leave your message on his answerphone, unless you do want to utterly humiliate him.

A nasty break: The e-mail method

Sending an e-mail is strictly for badly-behaved boys. It's a dead mean way of dumping someone, and who knows they may have the nerve to e-mail back for an explanation. If you really can't face him, write a letter and post it to him. It always seems more meaningful and heartfelt.

A good break: The honesty method

The hardest but fairest way of breaking up. Even if he makes your skin crawl you can still end up stumbling over your pre-prepared speech. Being honest about your feelings with him staring at you can be very difficult and painful for both of you but it may help you feel better about yourself. Pick a neutral location, preferably one near your best

135

mate's house for a dose of moral support after the event.

A gentle break: The 'It's me, not you' method

Taking the blame for your relationship melt-down can be a cool move. You're taking the boys on at their own game with this one: 'It's not your fault, it's me that's changed,' is a line guys love to use to take the heat off themselves. Let's be honest: it softens the blow and salvages their pride. And if you want to stay mates, then this is the one to use.

A painful break: The 'Let him guess' method

Another favourite tactic used by cowardly boys. If you opt for this, remember it can be a protracted, tiring battle of wits. You'll pick fights, you'll criticise him for the way he dresses, the way he acts, even the way he breathes, you'll never answer his calls. But be aware that this could take several long, agonising weeks until he gets sick of you and takes a hike.

A heartless break: The two-timing method

Secretly lining up another boy to take over as soon as you've plucked up the courage to drop boyfriend No.1 isn't a good move. You're not being honest with yourself, your boyfriend or your potential boyfriend, plus it makes you look bad and gives your ex justifiable ammunition if he's going to bad-mouth you. And hardly anyone'll stick up for a two-timer.

A pathetic break: The 'Let your mate tell him' method

This is a total cop-out, and totally disregards his feelings. It's even lower than sending an e-mail. Sending out the 'I'm a cold, heartless bitch' signal isn't likely to encourage potential suitors, is it?

HOW TO COPE WHEN YOU'RE DUMPED

Boys are terrible at finishing relationships; one of the reasons they desperately try to avoid getting involved in the first place is to avoid finding themselves in this very situation.

Almost without exception they'll go for the 'Let

her guess' method and/or the 'It's me, not you' method and if they're utter toerags, they'll opt for the 'Let your mate tell her' method.

Rachel, 17, from Manchester, remembers one method her boyfriend used to get the message across. 'Nigel, my boyfriend, opted for a novel approach once. He hid in his wardrobe whenever the phone rang rather than talk to a girl he was desperate to bin. Eventually his flatmate cottoned on to his "disappearing" act and forced him to put the poor girl out of her misery.'

You see, boys are cowards and find it difficult to cope with heavy, emotional situations. They don't want to upset you, but more importantly they don't want to play the role of the bad guy either.

But no matter what method he uses, it's horrible when you're dumped. If you reckon you're in love with him, it's a trauma you believe you'll never get over.

So before your mates start ignoring your morose moods, here's a few things that'll help you feel better:

1 – Get upset

You can't pretend you don't care and you can't control the strength of your feelings. You've been dumped, rejected; your confidence and dreams have been shattered, of course you're depressed. So cry, weep, wail and sob, it's very therapeutic.

2 – Get angry

You have every right to be very, very angry with your ex. Well, he dumped you and ruined everything, didn't he? After you've stamped on his pictures or ripped up a few of his possessions, writing 'I hate Doug (please put the appropriate name here), and I will get over him' a hundred times may do the trick. Or write a list of his good and bad points; you'll be surprised how imperfect he really is. Ultimately, relationships are all about having fun with someone you like and who isn't afraid to like you, too.

3 – Get a life

This is the final and most important one for mending a broken heart. Your friends are your salvation, so start going out with them and having a laugh. Focus on what you want to achieve in your life too, and start working towards the fulfilment of your dreams. It's a glorious world out there, filled with golden opportunities, and along the way you'll meet a few golden boys too.

Chapter 20

Q & A:
BOYS' DATING
FREAK-OUTS

Peer pressure

I get on really well with this girl and want to ask her out, but none of my mates like her. I'm really torn and don't know what to do?

Have you got a mind of your own? Of course you have. At the moment you're experiencing the negative effects of peer pressure. Every boy wants the approval of his mates but if it's going to affect your quality of life you need to ask yourself who you're going to put first, you or them. However you also need to ask yourself why they're against this girl; maybe there's something about her you're not aware of and they are. Ask them to be honest about their reasons, and you'll be a lot clearer about your next move.

Dial-a-date

I snogged a girl at a house party. I got her number but I'm too scared to phone her. What should I do?

The very fact that she gave you her phone number is fair indication she fancies you and wants you to call. You've already got the worst bit over with by snogging her already, haven't you? The longer you leave it the worse it'll be. And what if you bump into her before you've got round to calling her? She'll probably assume you're not into her. Give her a call, and immediately make a joke about how ridiculous you feel. She'll soon put you at ease. Remember, it's just as scary for her waiting to see if you'll ever get dialling.

Flirtathon

There's a girl I like who really flirts with me, but I think she's just being a tease. How can you tell when someone fancies you?

It sounds highly likely she's into you as teasing, singling you out for chats and full-on flirting is a pretty clear sign. Does she act the same way with other boys? If not, you could be on to a winner. If you're mates with her friends too, then ask them for their honest opinion, or get your mates to ask

141

them if you're too shy. Hopefully you'll discover she's not a terrible flirt, who gets off teasing boys and playing games with their hearts. Alternatively, the best way to deal with it is to talk to her and suss out if she's just as interested in you as you are in her.

Sex talk

I'm gagging to have sex with my girlfriend. Is there a good way of asking her?

You're entering an emotional and physical mine-field. Before you make any approach to your girl-friend, you firstly have to be truthful with yourself and the reasons why you're so desperate for sex. Do you respect and love her? Are you committed to your relationship? Is she over sixteen? Or is it because you're just curious, desperate to lose your virginity, all your mates are bragging about it or it's a combination of all of them? If you do think you're in love and committed to your girl, then you need to ask her if she's ready to take your relation-ship further. Be mature, discuss your feelings, con-traception and all the consequences of having sex, both emotionally and physically. If you do decide to go ahead, use a condom every single time.

CONCLUSION

ven if you do understand boys a bit better now, it's still easy enough to be confused by them. Try not to worry too much about this, because boys can act in bizarre ways sometimes. Over the years you'll make some brilliant boy mates and go out with some fantastic boyfriends too – but remember: don't count on one to make you: **a** happy, **b** popular or **c** complete. Only you can do this. Going out with a boy is about hanging out with someone who makes you feel good. But if you don't love or respect yourself then what hope has he got? So have a life, have a laugh and one day, sooner or later, you'll meet someone who'll love to be a part of your life too.

Good luck & enjoy yourself!

INDEX